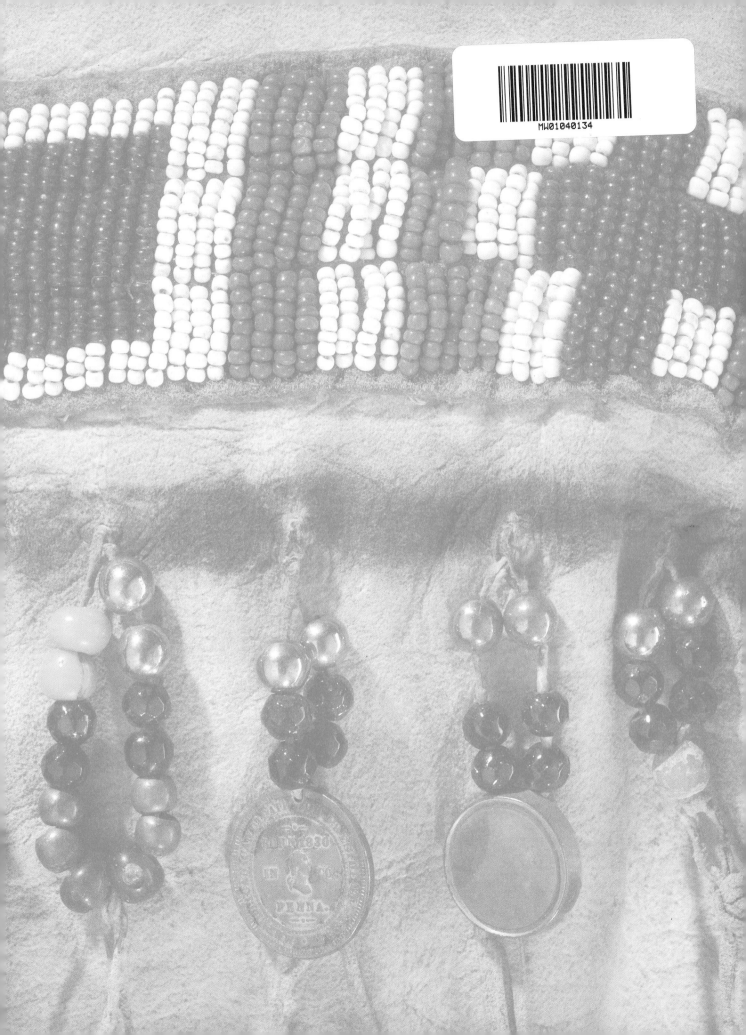

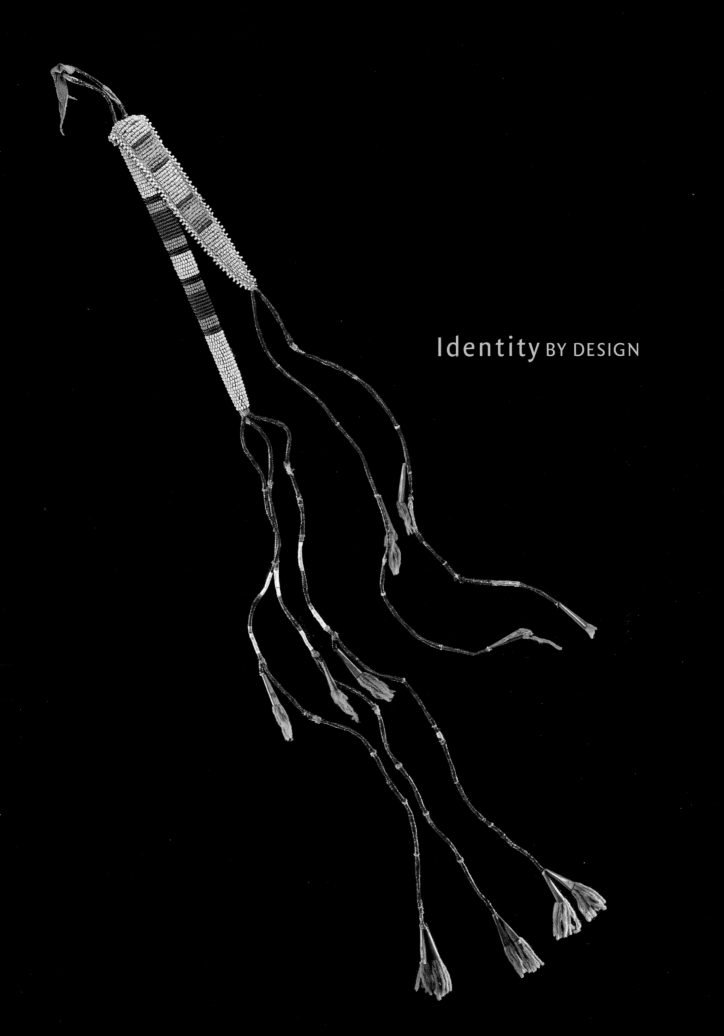

Identity BY DESIGN

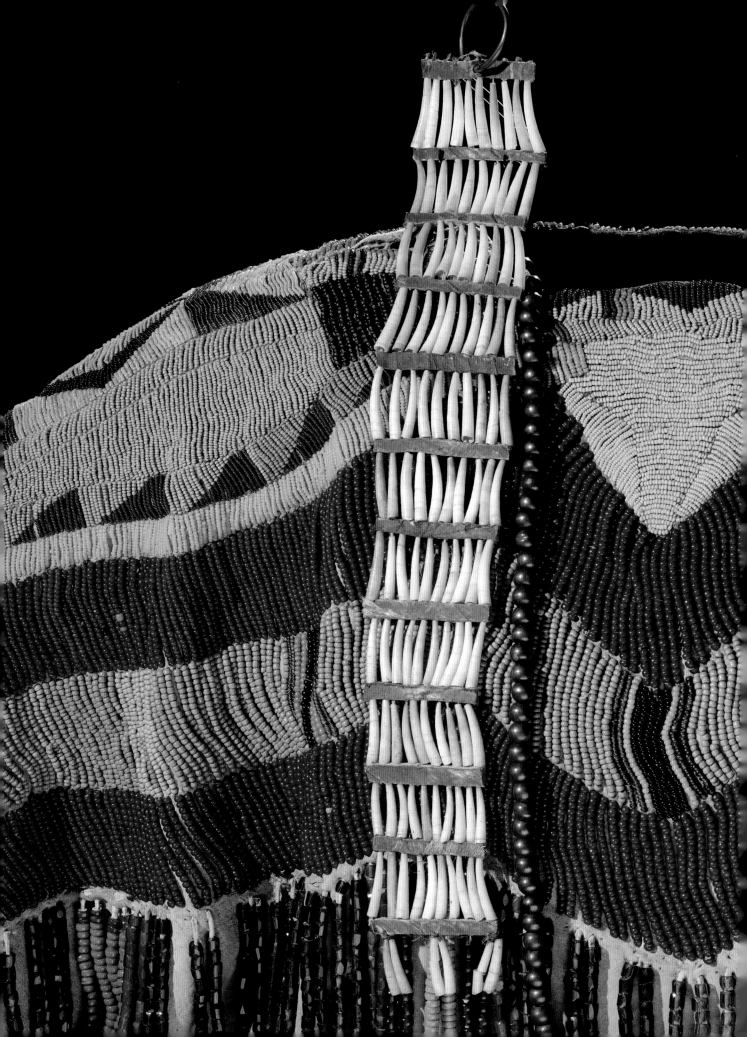

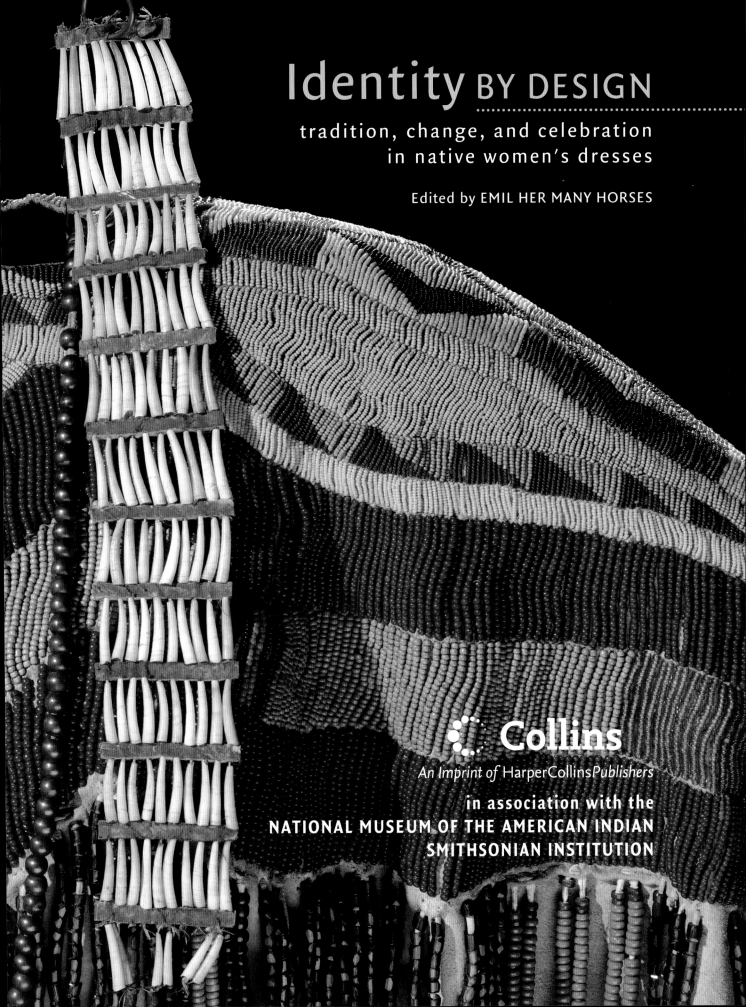

Identity BY DESIGN

tradition, change, and celebration
in native women's dresses

Edited by EMIL HER MANY HORSES

Collins

An Imprint of HarperCollinsPublishers

in association with the
NATIONAL MUSEUM OF THE AMERICAN INDIAN
SMITHSONIAN INSTITUTION

HarperCollins books may be purchased for educational, business, or sales promotional use. For information please write: Special Markets Department, HarperCollins Publishers, 10 East 53rd Street, New York, NY 10022.

FIRST EDITION

The name of the "Smithsonian," "Smithsonian Institution," and the sunburst logo are registered trademarks of the Smithsonian Institution.

Published in conjunction with the exhibition *Identity by Design: Tradition, Change, and Celebration in Native Women's Dresses*, opening at the Smithsonian's National Museum of the American Indian, Washington, D.C., in spring 2007. After its Washington showing, the exhibition opens in 2008 at NMAI's George Gustav Heye Center in New York City.

The National Museum of the American Indian, Smithsonian Institution, is dedicated to working in collaboration with the indigenous peoples of the Americas to foster and protect Native cultures throughout the Western Hemisphere. The museum's publishing program seeks to augment awareness of Native American beliefs and lifeways, and to educate the public about the history and significance of Native cultures.

National Museum of the American Indian
Project Director: Terence Winch, Head of Publications
Editor: Elizabeth Kennedy Gische
Designer: Steve Bell

Front cover: Crow elk tooth dress, ca. 1890. Montana. Red and green wool, imitation elk teeth (bone), seed beads, muslin, thread. 12/6406; Color lithograph of Alice Lone Bear (Sioux), 1898. Omaha, Nebraska. Photo by Frank A. Rinehart or Adolph F. Muhr. P11233

Back cover: Sioux side-fold dress (detail). See p. 23.

Page 1: Yankton Sioux beaded awl case, ca. 1880. Quill-wrapped fringe, tin cones, and yarn. 17/9737

Page 2: Crow Elk tooth dress (detail). See p. 36.

Page 3: Hunkpapa Lakota (Sioux) cloth dress (detail). See p. 50.

Page 4: Sioux two-hide pattern dress with fully beaded yoke, ca. 1865 (detail). See p. 44.

Page 5: Sioux two-hide pattern dress with fully beaded yoke, ca. 1900 (detail). See p. 100.

Pages 6–7: Yakama two-hide dress, earrings, and necklace (detail). See p. 31.

Page 9: White Mountain Apache girl's skirt (detail). See p. 71.

Library of Congress Cataloging-in-Publication Data

Identity by design : tradition, change, and celebration in Native women's dresses / edited by Emil Her Many Horses. — 1st ed.
     p. cm.
  Published in association with the National Museum of the American Indian, Smithsonian Institution.
  "Published in conjunction with the exhibition Identity by Design: Tradition, Change, and Celebration in Native Women's Dresses, opening at the Smithsonian's National Museum of the American Indian, Washington, D.C., in spring 2007"—T.p. verso.
  Includes bibliographical references and index.
  ISBN: 978-0-06-115369-3
  ISBN-10: 0-06-115369-9
  1. Indian women—Clothing—United States—Exhibitions. 2. Dresses—United States—Exhibitions. I. Her Many Horses, Emil. II. National Museum of the American Indian (U.S.)

E98.W8I34 2007
746.9'208997—dc22

2006049750

10 9 8 7 6 5 4 3 2 1

Contents

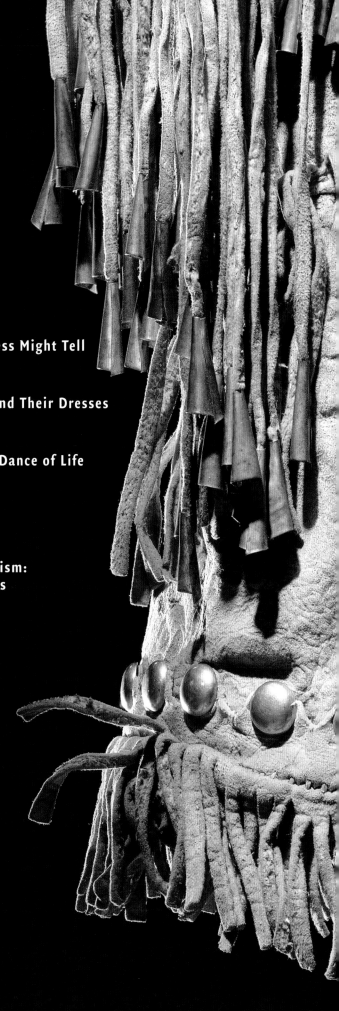

11   FOREWORD: **The Story the Dress Might Tell**
W. RICHARD WEST, JR.

15   **Portraits of Native Women and Their Dresses**
EMIL HER MANY HORSES

65   **Dresses, Designers, and the Dance of Life**
COLLEEN CUTSCHALL

95   **The Invisible Dress**
ELIZABETH WOODY

97   **Creativity and Cosmopolitanism:
Women's Enduring Traditions**
JANET CATHERINE BERLO

149   **Contributors**

152   **Photo Credits**

154   **Index**

The Story the Dress Might Tell

IDENTITY BY DESIGN: *Tradition, Change, and Celebration in Native Women's Dresses* shows us clearly that dresses are much more than simple articles of clothing for Native women—they are complex expressions of culture and identity. Often made from such organic materials as deerhide and elk teeth, and infused with the spirit of its maker, a dress can seem to take on a life of its own. I am reminded of a remark made by Rebecca Lyon, an Athabaskan/Alutiiq artist, who worked with us on a recent project: "Nothing is as personal as the clothes we wear. Clothing can be seen as a vessel that holds the human spirit."

As Director of the National Museum of the American Indian, I have had the somewhat ironic mission of stressing that our extraordinary collections of Native objects—some 800,000 works of astounding beauty and value—are secondary to the cultural significance these objects hold for Native people. What I mean is that our institution is fundamentally more cultural center than museum, more a locus of living cultures than "a cabinet of curiosities." The objects we are privileged to care for are not ends in themselves, but ways for us to understand and appreciate the evolving identity of Native people and communities in all their multiple dimensions. Our rich collection of dresses and dress accessories from the Plains, Plateau, and Great Basin that you will learn about in this book and its related exhibition illustrate perfectly the ways in which an object of stunning aesthetic qualities can transcend its own beauty to become a metaphor for a multitude of deeper meanings.

Consider, if you will, the last stanza of a wonderful poem called "She Dances" by Heid E. Erdrich, a member of both the Turtle Mountain Band of Ojibway and one of Native America's most distinguished literary families:

Cheyenne three-hide dress (detail). See p. 56.

But I once dreamed my friend a dress:
one in slipping honey colors of satin
with black bands. Its music came with
its cones jangling and flashing near each
flower-print cloth outfit then on to the next.
And now I dream her another dress,
the one for labor, a traditional: deep blue,
the midnight wool blue shot with red
that all her ancestors would recognize,
the heavy dress of history,
the one made of flags
and ration blankets and blood.

When I came across this poem very recently, I was immediately struck by how artfully Heid has synthesized contemporary attitude and language with time-honored tradition and belief. Even non-Natives, I think, can get a real feel here for the way in which the idea for a dress, and the story the dress might tell, are every bit as important as the tangible dress itself. The one verse has it all: the contemporary importance of the dress, the abiding presence of the ancestors, and the historical narrative embodied in the work.

The museum is grateful to all the contemporary artists who shared their knowledge and experiences with us, greatly enriching the exhibition and this book. We particularly thank project consultants Joyce Growing Thunder Fogarty (Assiniboine/Sioux), Juanita Growing Thunder Fogarty (Assiniboine/Sioux), Gladys Jefferson (Crow), Keri Jhane Myers (Comanche), Jamie Okuma (Luiseño/Shoshone-Bannock), and Jackie Parsons (Blackfeet). Many other dress designers and dancers also generously shared their insights with us, including Rebecca Brady (Cheyenne/Sac and Fox), Jodi Gillette (Hunkpapa Lakota), Vanessa Jennings (Kiowa), and Georgianna Old Elk (Assiniboine).

We are indebted to Colleen Cutschall (Oglala Lakota) and my colleague Emil Her Many Horses (Oglala Lakota), who served as exemplary co-curators of the exhibition and as essayists in this book, of which Emil is the editor. We also owe thanks to Janet Catherine Berlo for her fine essay in the volume. A poem by Elizabeth Woody (Warm Springs-Yakama/Navajo) adds a luminous grace note.

This book would not have been produced without the commitment of the NMAI Publications Office, especially head of publications Terence Winch and managing editor Ann Kawasaki. Editor Elizabeth Kennedy Gische and designer Steve Bell, assisted by interns Guy Flagg and Amanda Theis, dedicated their enviable talents to the book. Photographers Ernest Amoroso, Walter Larrimore, and R. A. Whiteside of the museum's Office of Photo Services, headed by Cynthia Frankenburg, took the beautiful color photographs of the dresses and accessories that adorn the book. Lou Stancari contributed photo research.

For the exhibition, project manager Wayne Smith and exhibit manager Jennifer Tozer ably guided a dedicated team. Eric Christiansen designed the gallery spaces, and Chris Arnold handled design of the Family Room, working closely with education specialists Vilma Ortiz-Sanchez, Pamela Woodis (Jicarilla Apache), and Suzanne Davis. Elizabeth Hunter designed the exhibit graphics. Kate Mitchell edited the exhibition script. Monica Sanjur was responsible for production of exhibit graphics and Levia Lew for lighting design. Thanks are due to Rick Pelasara and the museum's production shop for exhibition fabrication. Susan Heald and Anna Hodson performed conservation work on the dresses and accessories, and Shelly Uhlir and Robert Patterson were responsible for mountmaking. Fran Biehl, Thomas Evans (Pawnee), and Erik Satrum provided essential collections support. We thank Kathy Suter and Dan Davis for media development and production, and Linda Martin (Navajo) for her work on public programs for the exhibition. Jason Wigfield and Cheryl Wilson handled website coverage for *Identity by Design*. We are grateful also to Justin Giles (Muscogee Creek) for community services work for the exhibition, and to Amy Drapeau and Maggie Bertin, Virginia Elwell, and Gina Ward for public relations and development support.

Finally, on behalf of the museum, I express my heartfelt gratitude to Margaret A. Cargill, whose quiet generosity helped make this, and many other projects, possible. For the past decade, Miss Cargill was our museum's anonymous benefactor, and we are all saddened by her passing. In closing, let me also express my sincere thanks to the International Music and Art Foundation for its support of *Identity by Design*.

—W. RICHARD WEST, JR.
(Southern Cheyenne and member of the Cheyenne and Arapaho Tribes of Oklahoma)
Founding Director, National Museum of the American Indian

Portraits of Native Women and Their Dresses

SITTING IN THE AUDIENCE AT THE TRIBAL FUSIONS FASHION SHOW sponsored by the Institute of American Indian Arts during the annual Indian Art Market in Santa Fe, New Mexico, in 2005, I listened as noted Kiowa author N. Scott Momaday read from his book *The Way to Rainy Mountain* during the opening of the event:

East of my grandmother's house, south of the pecan grove, there is buried a woman in a beautiful dress. Mammedaty [Momaday's grand-father] used to know where she is buried, but now no one knows. If you stand on the front porch of the house and look eastward toward Carnegie, you know that the woman is buried somewhere within the range of your vision. But her grave is unmarked. She was buried in a cabinet, and she wore a beautiful dress. How beautiful it was! It was one of those fine buckskin dresses, and it was decorated with elk's teeth and beadwork. That dress is still there, under the ground. [1]

As I reflected on the powerful image of the woman and her dress evoked by Momaday, I couldn't help but think of the stories my grandmothers told me about the dresses they once owned. Both women were from the Oglala Lakota Nation (one of the seven branches of the Teton subdivision of the Sioux) from South Dakota. They lived far to the north of Carnegie, Oklahoma, and their dress styles were quite different from those described by Momaday—yet no less beautiful.

"Why did mama let me sell my dress? I was crazy!" my maternal grandmother, Grace Pourier, recalled regretfully. "They said there was a woman down at the agency buying beadwork, and I asked mama if I could sell my dress, and she said 'Okay.'"

Born in 1909, my grandmother was the daughter of Emil and Emma (Lee) Pourier and granddaughter of Baptiste and Josephine (Richards) Pourier. The Indian agency where she parted with her cherished dress—made for her, the oldest grandchild, by "Grandma Pourier"—was located on the Oglala Lakota reservation at Pine Ridge, South Dakota. The only remaining evidence of the dress is a family photo of my grandmother, as a child, wearing the wonderful garment (see p. 16).

The dress had a fully beaded yoke (the piece of the dress that is fitted around the neck and shoulders) and was made of tanned hide (also called buckskin). This style of dress was the height of fashion among the Lakota after 1870, during the time that Native people began to be confined to reservations and reserves in both the United States and Canada. "My dress was beaded with cut glass beads!" my grandmother would exclaim. Faceted glass beads known as cut beads were introduced in the early 1900s. When light hits these beads in a certain way, they appear to sparkle—a characteristic that makes cut beads popular to this day. My grandmother wore a pair of fully beaded leggings and moccasins with the dress, and she explained, "The soles of the moccasins were fully beaded." Some people believe that moccasins of this type are burial moccasins. Annabelle One Star, a relative of my grandmother and a renowned Oglala beadworker who married into a Sicangu family on South Dakota's Rosebud Reservation, explained that she also had a pair of moccasins with beaded soles made for her as a young girl. ("They were difficult to walk in, especially on a hardwood floor," she remembered.) Annabelle, like my grandmother, lived a good, long life, which would certainly challenge the belief that moccasins with fully beaded soles were burial moccasins.

"I fought them for my dress." The voice of my paternal grandmother, Emily Her Many Horses, was full of emotion as she told me the story of how she had been forced to part with her dress, which had been made of wool and decorated with elk teeth. The elk teeth that adorned such a dress are still highly prized, as they are the eyeteeth (only two per elk) and are a natural ivory. At my grandmother's naming ceremony—an occasion at which it is traditional for the family of the person being named to give away gifts—her parents, Susie (Blunt Horn) and Louis Mathews, made her change out of her dress and give it away.

"I wondered why my grandpa had my shoes tied to his saddle," my grandmother remembered. After they wrestled the dress off my grandmother and gave it away, my great-great-grandfather John Blunt Horn gave away five horses in her honor that day.

My grandmothers' dresses are probably still out in the world somewhere, perhaps part of a museum collection or treasured as another family's heirloom, but memories of these women and their dresses remain with me—how one grandmother regretted having sold her dress, and the other lamented not fighting hard enough to save hers. Such dresses were created with love by grandmothers, worn for special occasions such as a ceremony or a dance, and sometimes saved so one could be buried in her finest. They reflect the creativity of dressmakers who followed styles developed and passed down by past generations of Native artists. With the introduction of new trade materials, dress styles evolved, but remained within specific tribal styles created by societies dedicated to quillwork and, later, beadwork.

IDENTITY BY DESIGN

Identity by Design: Tradition, Change, and Celebration in Native Women's Dresses draws upon the National Museum of the American Indian's renowned collection of dresses from the Plains, Plateau, and Great Basin regions of the United States and Canada to explore the last 200 years of Native women's clothing and design. The dresses—along with the words, insights, and memories of contemporary women artists who design and make dresses—reveal that Native women's clothing, then and now, reflects tribal and family traditions and individual artistic skill and expression.

In December 2005, the National Museum of the American Indian (NMAI) invited six Native women artists from the Plains, Plateau, and Great Basin to view the museum's dress collection and discuss indigenous clothing. Additional dress designers and dancers also generously shared their knowledge. The wisdom and experiences of these artists—from Jackie Parsons' description of the women's War Bonnet Society to Keri Jhane Myers' account of her forays into New York City's Fashion District—greatly enrich this book. In the pages to follow, I examine the development and evolution of three popular dress styles: the side-fold dress, the two-hide dress, and the three-hide dress.

In preparation for the exhibition *Identity by Design: Tradition, Change, and Celebration in Native Women's Dresses*, the National Museum of the American Indian invited six celebrated Native women artists whose many skills include designing dresses to visit the museum in December 2005 and discuss its dress collection and the art of dressmaking. From left to right: Jamie Okuma (Luiseño/Shoshone-Bannock), Gladys Jefferson (Crow), Joyce Growing Thunder Fogarty (Assiniboine/Sioux), Jackie Parsons (Blackfeet), Keri Jhane Myers (Comanche), and Juanita Growing Thunder Fogarty (Assiniboine/Sioux).

The garment worn in the historic portrait by Karl Bodmer (opposite page) helped inspire the design of a dress created by Jodi Gillette (Hunkpapa Lakota). A renowned Northern Women's Traditional dancer from North Dakota, she danced in the dress at the NMAI National Pow-wow at the MCI (Verizon) Center in Washington, D.C., August 2005 (left, and opposite page, right).

SIDE-FOLD DRESS

As its name indicates, the side-fold dress was created by wrapping a large animal skin around the body and sewing a seam up one side.[2] Popular in the early 1800s, they were worn by Native women of the Upper Missouri River region, on the northeastern Plains, and in the western Great Lakes region.

When I interviewed Jodi Gillette, a dressmaker from the Hunkpapa and Oglala Lakota nations, at NMAI's 2005 National Powwow in Washington, D.C., I asked how she came up with the design of her dress, particularly the cut of the skirt (see p. 20). "I saw an image of a painting showing the corner section of a dress's skirt adorned with what appeared to be beaded rows," she replied. "That's why I cut the skirt of my dress with tabs and decorated it with beaded rows."[3] The image Gillette refers to is a portrait of a Teton Sioux woman named Chan-Chä-Uiá-Teüin by Swiss artist Karl Bodmer, who encountered her in 1833 (see below, left). The portrait may be the only extant painting known to illustrate a side-fold dress.[4] The early style that Gillette chose to research is a dress fashion that I believe not many contemporary Lakota dressmakers would realize was once a Sioux style of dress.

Karl Bodmer (Swiss, 1809–1893), *Chan-Chä-Uiá-Teüin, Teton Sioux Woman*, 1833–39. Watercolor and pencil on paper, 43.2 x 30.2 cm. Joslyn Art Museum, Omaha, Nebraska, Gift of the Enron Art Foundation, 1986. JAM1986.49.246

The National Museum of the American Indian holds one of eleven known side-fold dresses in museum collections. George Gustav Heye (1874–1957), founder of NMAI's predecessor institution, the Museum of the American Indian/Heye Foundation, purchased the dress in 1911 from W. O. Oldman, a seller in London, England. The side-fold dress is documented in NMAI records by Heye as Plains Cree, but Norman Feder, who conducted research that compared documented specimens in Berlin's Museum für Völkerkunde and the Brooklyn Museum, concluded in 1965 that this dress is Eastern Sioux.[5]

Rosemary Lessard's description of a sideseam or side-fold dress fits the NMAI side-fold: "If one folded down the top quarter of a quilled robe, wrapped it around the wearer and sewed up the open side, the process would produce a garment closely resembling the sideseam dresses that are now in museum collections."[6] The NMAI side-fold dress (see p. 23) is unique in that it has long extensions from the upper cape portion of the dress that appear to be formed from the legs of a large animal hide; other known side-fold dresses lack these extensions.

The rows of porcupine quillwork on NMAI's dress resemble those sewn on a quilled robe and indicate that the person who made the dress was a member of a quillwork society—a group that monitored the production of quillwork— and that the dressmaker had obtained the knowledge to do quillwork from another member of the quillwork society or from a dream.[7] For the Lakota, the rows of quillwork would symbolize "the trail on which woman travels."[8] The

Opposite far right and below: Sioux side-fold dress, ca. 1830. Probably South Dakota. Hide, pony beads, porcupine quills, tin cones, cloth, sinew. 2/9801

Opposite near right: Diagram of a side-fold dress.

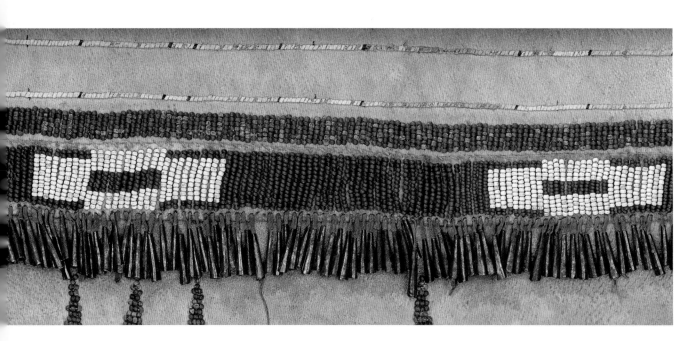

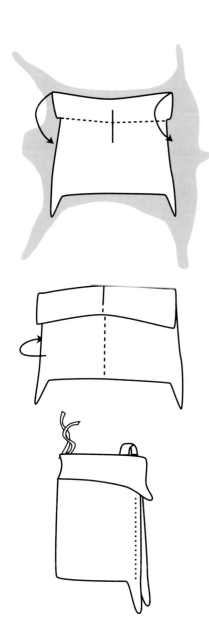

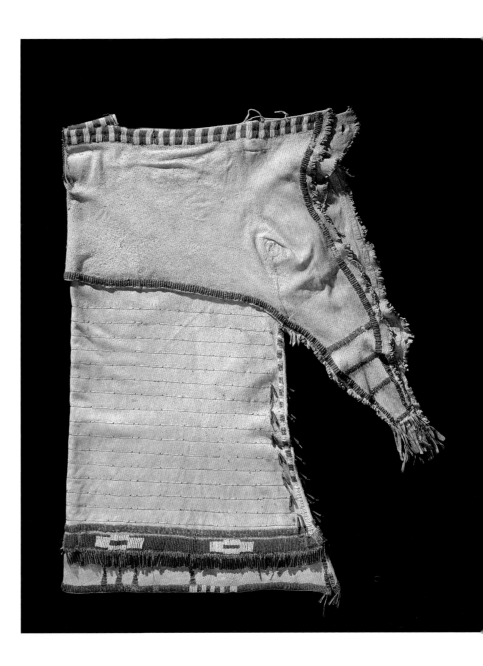

soft colors of the quills reveal that they were dyed by using natural colors as opposed to aniline dyes later introduced by traders.

The NMAI side-fold dress is decorated with blue and white glass pony beads. The first glass beads introduced by non-Native traders to the Northern Plains in the 1800s were called "pony beads" because they were transported by pony pack trains.[9] Blue beads were popular because the color was rare in Indian dye sources.[10] The combination of the traditional art of quillwork with the use of trade goods on this dress indicates that the skilled artist was a person of high social status whose family was able to trade for valuable materials.

Sioux side-fold dress (detail). See p. 23.

The tin cones fashioned from metal trade objects that embellish the dress replace carved dew claws taken from deer hooves that were previously used by Native dressmakers.[11] Jodi Gillette explained one reason why dew claws or, later, tin cones, were attached to dresses:

> People wore jingly things at the bottom of their dresses, so that others could hear them when they were coming. Usually, we had strong protocols about being around our fathers-in-law or certain other members of the family—you weren't really supposed to talk with them or be alone with them. The noise signaled to other people that you were approaching, so they could react properly, either by leaving or getting somebody like a grandmother to be in the room or in the same area.

Small pieces of red cloth peek out from inside the tin cones that embellish the side-fold dress in NMAI's collection. Woolen fabric was an important item introduced by Euro-American traders and quickly adapted by Native dressmakers. Expensive at first, the cloth was initially used by dressmakers as decoration rather than for the basic material of clothing.[12]

The cut of the side-fold would make it prohibitive for a woman to ride astride a horse, and this style of dress was worn when women were living a more sedentary lifestyle. The side-fold dress style depicted in the portrait that influenced Jodi Gillette's creation was near the end of its popularity when Karl Bodmer painted Chan-Chä-Uiá-Teüin.

INDIGENOUS INVENTION

Native people traded and incorporated new materials into their lives long before the arrival of Europeans in North America. Extensive intertribal trade networks supplied women with highly prized goods such as dentalium shells, elk teeth, beads made from shells, and paints, which they used to ornament dresses or trade as goods.

In the 1700s, English, French, Russian, and Spanish traders and soldiers introduced European trade materials to Native peoples during a period of fierce competition for fur trade and military alliances.[13] Women found innovative ways to adapt these materials to their dresses, blending old with new; while some refused to use these materials as a sign of resistance to European influence.[14]

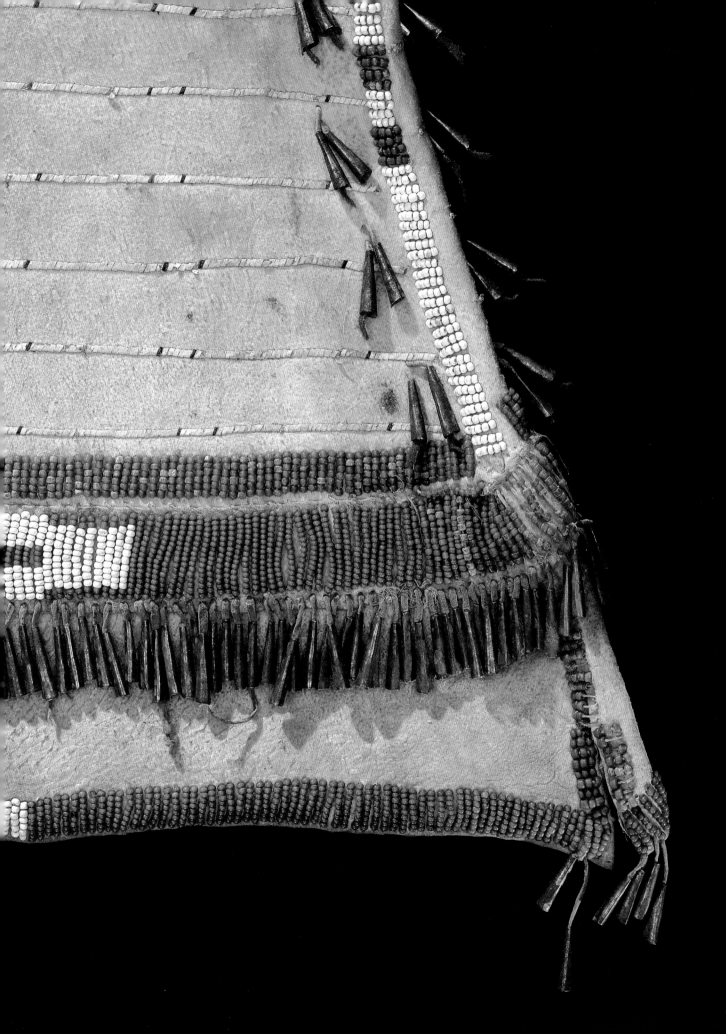

Kiowa cloth dress, ca. 1900. Oklahoma. Saved-list blue wool, seed beads, red wool, muslin, thread. 2/2154

Native women sewed cloth dresses that incorporated the white edge or "saved-list" of the fabric as decoration along the sleeves and bottoms. European tailors usually cut off and discarded this undyed material. The designer of this dress added tapered side panels (see the longer hemline at the sides) to represent animal legs, a common feature of hide dresses.

The combination of trade—both intertribal and European—and women's experimental attitude toward artistic expression ensured that the region's dresses were aesthetically diverse and continually evolving.

BEADS

Before European contact, Native people made beads from shell, bone, stone, and other natural materials. After Europeans arrived in the area, most of the beads traded to tribes by French, English, Russian, and Spanish traders were made in Italy.[15] The increasing availability of trade beads made it almost inevitable that artists would replace quillwork with beadwork. Beads did not require the labor of washing or dyeing.

The earliest European trade beads—which arrived in the western Great Lakes region about 1675[16] and would eventually reach the Plains by the 1800s—were the large pony beads. Around 1850, a smaller bead, referred to as a "seed bead," was introduced. This marked the start of a new period in beadwork, as the smaller-sized beads enabled dressmakers to do elaborate work that covered more of the dress.

INDIAN CLOTH

When introduced to woolen cloth by European traders, women used it only sparingly on dresses. Later, when hides became less available due to the decimation of animal herds by Euro-American hunters and the lack of hunting opportunities caused by the confinement of tribes to reservations, cloth—which had become more plentiful—was used to make dresses that resembled those of hide, could be decorated in much the same way, and were easier to make.

The Gloucestershire region of England produced most of the woolen cloth for the Indian trade. Known as "saved-list," "stroud," or "Indian" cloth, it often came in dark blue or scarlet. The term "saved-list" refers to the cloth's undyed lists or edges. Even after less expensive dyes were developed around 1850, manufacturers continued to make these white-edged woolen cloths to meet the demand of Native women. As woolen trade cloth dresses began to slowly replace hide dresses, Native dressmakers ingeniously used the white edge or "saved-list" to decorate the ends of sleeves and the bottoms of dresses. European tailors usually cut off and discarded this material.[17]

TWO-HIDE DRESS

By the early 1830s, two-hide dress patterns were in fashion. Made by matching two hides of deer, elk, or bighorn sheep, "the full skirted two-skin dress was the ideal solution to the new way of travel on horseback."[18] The tail of the animal was left intact on each hide, and, along with a section of the hind legs of the hides, would be folded over, forming a yoke or cape at the shoulders of the dress. The tail was the central design in the front and back of the dress just below the opening of the neck when the hides were sewn together. Early examples of this style, such as the Arikara dress pictured on the opposite page, were simply decorated with earth paints. According to Richard Conn, this style of dress can be found "among the Sarsi, Blackfeet, Crow, Assiniboine, Dakota, Mandan, Hidatsa, and Iowa of the Plains, and among the Yakama, Flathead, Kutenai, Okanogan, Sanpoil, Nez Perce and Wishram in the Plateau. Since 1890, the Plains-type … has diffused over most of North America."[19] Among dressmakers of the Plateau, for two-hide dresses, sometimes called "tail dresses," the "skins of female animals were preferred, as the wearer was believed to acquire certain properties of the animal whose skin she wore."[20]

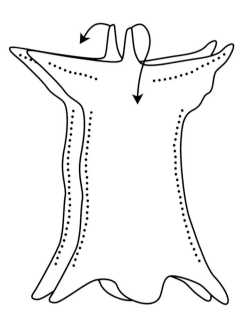

Diagram of a two-hide dress.

Arikara two-hide dress, ca. 1840. North Dakota. Bighorn sheep hide, blue-green and red paint, sinew. 12/8931

The two-hide style is still popular among tribes of the Plateau region, which stretches from British Columbia south to the northern half of Idaho and into northwestern Montana. With Plateau-style dresses, pony beads did not go out of style, making it difficult to date these dresses. (Objects in museum collections are commonly dated according to the materials used in their creation.) Some dress yokes show several types of beads, including pony beads, seed beads, and cut glass beads. Plateau dresses are also characterized by rows of leather fringes decorated with trade beads called "Russian" or "Siberian" beads (see pp. 30, 31). Such beads were likely "not made in Russia, but were carried by Russian traders to the west coast of North America, subsequently moving eastward via intertribal trade," Lois Sherr Dubin observes in *The History of Beads: From 30,000 B.C. to the Present*. "These beads may have been acquired by the Russians in China (where they had been imported from Europe) and brought to the Northwest coast as part of the fur trade."[21]

Jamie Okuma, a member of the Shoshone/Bannock and the Luiseño, notes that people from the Great Basin—which includes the southern parts of Oregon and Idaho, all of Nevada and Utah, and the western halves of Wyoming

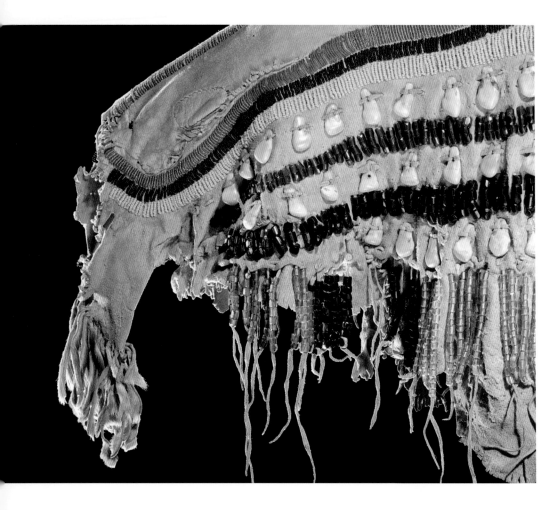

Left: Yakama two-hide dress (detail). See p. 103.

Below: Yakama purse, ca. 1910. Washington. Corn husk, yarn, hide. 22/8995

Opposite: Yakama two-hide dress, ca. 1890. Washington. Hide, pony beads, faceted "Russian" glass beads, fire-polished glass beads, cut glass beads, seed beads, sinew. 14/3568; Yakama basket hat, ca. 1910. Washington. Plant materials, seed beads, thread. 23/726; Yakama earrings, ca. 1910. Washington. Brass hoops, dentalium shells, red-painted rawhide. 20/4297; Yakama necklace, ca. 1930. Washington. Brass beads, leather. 13/7892

Extensive beadwork such as that on this dress is found on many Plateau dresses today. The animals' tails have been replaced by beadwork, and even the fringe is beaded. The colored beads strung on the fringe of this dress and that pictured above left are called "Russian" beads. This Yakama artist also chose to incorporate beads from many different time periods.

The award-winning artist
began beading at a very
early age and through-
out high school made
powwow dresses
for herself and
friends.
"After my first
powwow when I
was five at my grand-
mother's reservation,
that was it for me," she
says. "Seeing all the outfits really pushed me to
do beadwork. The pow-
wow experience when I
was younger was the best
thing I could have ever
done or had my family
involve me in."

Shoshone two-hide
pattern dress with fully
beaded yoke, ca. 1880.
Colorado. Hide, seed
beads, red wool, sinew.
1/8279; Shoshone belt, ca.
1910. Colorado. Canvas,
seed beads, thread,
leather tie. 23/2984;
Shoshone moccasins
and leggings, ca. 1890.
Colorado. Hide,
rawhide, seed beads,
sinew. 18/5928

The Shoshone were con-
sidered intermediaries in
the region's elaborate
intertribal trading net-
work. As a result, they
borrowed ideas from
tribes with whom they
had regular commerce,
mainly those of the
Northern Plains. This
Shoshone artist's dress
resembles a Sioux-style
dress because of the
fully beaded yoke.

and Colorado—were influenced by many sources: "When I look at Shoshone/Bannock dresses, some are distinctive. But the Shoshone are a very eclectic tribe, and they collect many different styles" (see p. 32). As Susan Jennys observed, "During the nineteenth century, clothing styles among many Shoshone and Nez Perce and, to a limited extent, some Ute bands, were quite similar to those Plains tribes such as the Crow, Northern Arapaho, and Western Sioux."[22]

Two-hide dresses from the Blackfeet (Southern Piegan) of Northern Montana and related tribes of the Blackfoot Confederacy of Canada held by the NMAI illustrate the style of ornamentation common from 1850 to 1880. Pony beads follow the contour of animal hide on the yoke of the dress. Blackfeet dressmakers added a unique element to their dresses in the elaborated decoration of the skirt, as seen in the dress on pp. 34, 35. The V-shaped ornament of red and blue wool attached to the skirt symbolizes the head of the animal, while red and blue wool inserts at the lower edge of the skirt represent the kidneys of the animal.[23] Along with the use of the tail, these designs pay respect to the animal whose hide is used to make the dress. The limited use of wool on these dresses speaks to the expense of the material.

Jackie Parsons, a Blackfeet artist and dressmaker from Browning, Montana, speaks of the decline of traditional dresses among her people: "Many of the dresses have disappeared because of deaths. Women are being buried in their dresses. Nobody was picking up the traditional making of Blackfeet dresses in buckskin or cloth." Due to the accomplishments of artists like Parsons, however, these arts are being revived.

Blackfoot two-hide dress, ca. 1860. Canada. Hide, pony beads, glass trade beads, seed beads, black and yellow paint, red and blue wool, sinew. 13/2381

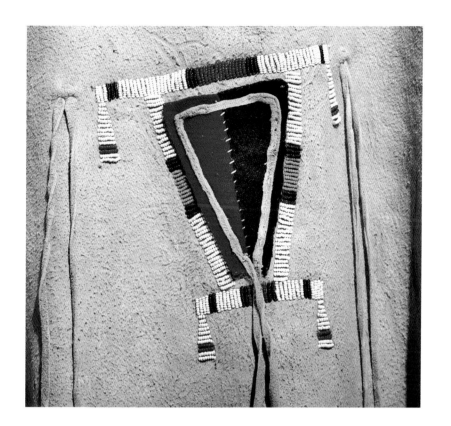

Crow elk tooth dress, ca. 1900. Montana. Hide, imitation elk teeth (bone), seed beads, red wool, sinew. 14/3597

Crow artists design dresses for special occasions that are often adorned with elk teeth or, in this case, imitation elk teeth carved from bone. The V-neck on the dress recalls the tail on an historic two-hide dress, but the closed, tapered sleeves are an innovation.

TWO-HIDE TRANSITIONAL STYLE DRESS

As new materials were introduced, dress styles evolved yet maintained a foundation derived from the two-hide dress. Crow dressmakers developed several features in their dresses that one might not identify as belonging to a true two-hide pattern, such as tapered sleeves, which are cut from a separate hide and sewn to the body of the dress. The tapered sleeves are sewn closed. In addition, a cloth panel is cut out of wool and attached to the neck opening of the dress to represent the tail section of the original two-hide dress.[24] The dress decoration consists of rows of lazy-stitch beadwork (a method of beading in rows sometimes called "lane stitch") and rows of elk teeth (see below and p. 36). A large number of elk teeth on a dress indicated that the wearer's husband was a skilled hunter or had the means to trade for the teeth. Elk teeth represented longevity because when other parts of an elk decayed, the ivory teeth remained.

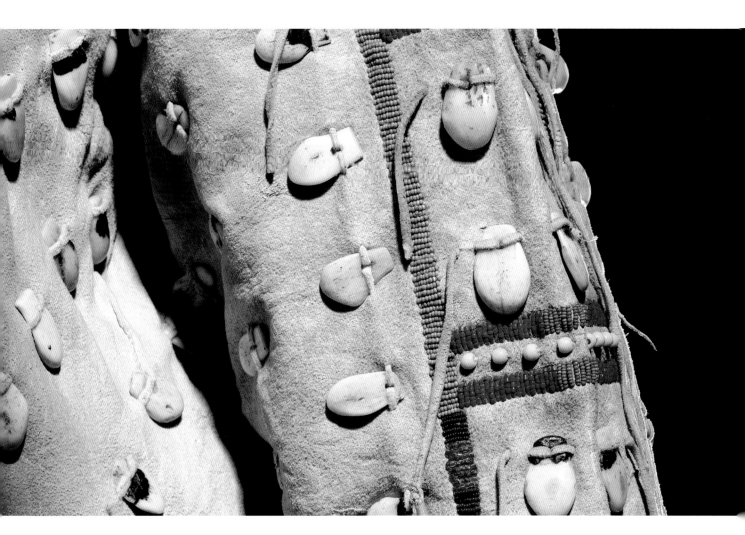

Crow Fair celebrants on
horseback, Montana,
2004.

Crow women on horse-
back with cross-lances
and shields, wearing
buckskin elk tooth dresses
in front of dance house,
ca. 1900. Photo by Willem
Wildschut. P22476

Women parading in their elk tooth dresses at Crow Fair, Montana, 1996.

As elk became scarce and hunting opportunities were limited after the Crow were confined to reservations, the teeth attached to many Crow dresses were carved out of bone. Today, many of the "teeth" that embellish elk tooth dresses are commercially made of plastic, although natural teeth are still preferred.

This style of elk tooth dress with tapered sleeves is still popular today, but they are now made from trade cloth, and the hide dresses are mostly decorated with colored rows of lazy-stitch beadwork. Crow women wear their beautiful dresses of hide and trade cloth during the annual Crow Fair celebration (see above and p. 38). Crow Fair is held the third weekend in August at Crow Agency, Montana. On the fourth day of the celebration, the Crow people dance throughout the camp. "We dance around the whole camp," dressmaker and dancer Gladys Jefferson explains. "We stop four times, for the four seasons. At the downbeat of the drum, while the people are parade-dancing, they wave to the mountains to bring a good winter and game. We make wishes for a good year ... elk tooth dresses are worn on that day."

Sioux dresses also have their foundation in the two-hide dress pattern. The dress pictured on p. 40, for example, was collected from the Sioux around 1850. The dress has the deer tails intact and is decorated with rows of elk teeth and elaborately adorned with pony beads. Such a valuable dress would have been worn by a young girl from a prominent family. As pony beads became more abundant, Sioux dressmakers enhanced their creativity by not only beading the cape of two-hide dresses but also replacing the animal tail with a symbolic beaded U-shaped design (see p. 42). With the introduction of the smaller seed beads, by the 1870s Sioux dresses were being fashioned with fully beaded yokes. At this point, however, three hides were used to produce a dress—one for the yoke or cape and two for the skirt. The overall dress pattern nonetheless still reflected that of the two-hide pattern dress.

Having grown up on the Rosebud and Pine Ridge reservations in South Dakota and attended dances at both, I can tell you that only a few fully beaded yoke dresses remain on the reservations. Most of the dresses were family heirlooms, and occasionally a young woman would wear her grandmother's dress at one of the annual fairs. Since the 1960s, dance competitions at powwows have become highly popular, including a category called "Women's Traditional" that requires a traditional-style dress or outfit. Fully beaded yoke dresses have today become a standard dress for the Women's Traditional dance category. Some contemporary dressmakers create dresses that follow the traditional style of a hide dress with the yoke fully beaded, while others make dresses with only the border of the yoke beaded or left entirely plain. With so few examples of traditional hide dresses left, some dressmakers freely interpret the cut of the yoke and bead designs. I know that many of the dressmakers today are researching published examples of dresses and studying museum collections—and, of course, consulting their elders—before creating a dress.

Opposite: Sioux girl's two-hide dress, ca. 1850. South Dakota. Deerhide, elk teeth, pony beads, red wool, sinew. 5/3776

This dress is decorated with 150 elk teeth. The number of elk teeth is a sign of the wealth of the girl's family. Since only the eyeteeth of the elk (two per elk) are used on dresses, her relatives may have been excellent hunters and/or traders.

O-o-be (Kiowa) wearing a three-hide dress decorated with elk teeth, 1895. Fort Sill, Oklahoma. Photographer unknown. P13149

Sioux two-hide dress (transitional style), ca. 1855. Probably South Dakota. Deerhide, pony beads, "hawk" brass bells, sinew. 15/9288

In the mid 1800s, Sioux women began replacing the animal's tail on a two-hide dress with a beaded U-shaped design. With the greater availability of trade beads, artists could be more creative and experiment with new designs. Here, the crosses on the yoke may represent the Four Directions or the Morning Star.

Joyce Growing Thunder Fogarty (Assiniboine/Sioux) and her daughter Juanita, 2005. Joyce is a traditional beadworker and the only artist ever to win Best of Show three times at Santa Fe Indian Market. Juanita has also won numerous awards at Santa Fe Indian Market, including the Best of Classification for bead- and quillwork in 2005. Like her mother, Juanita uses traditional Assiniboine designs in her art. When doing quillwork, Juanita follows the traditional approach, softening the porcupine quill in her mouth and flattening it with her teeth before attaching the quill to hide or cloth.

Present-day dressmakers (and mother and daughter) Joyce and Juanita Growing Thunder Fogarty (Assiniboine/Sioux) have had the opportunity not only to research dresses in museum collections but also to see relatives produce dresses on their home reservation, Fort Peck Indian Reservation in Poplar, Montana. Juanita explains about the further evolution of the U-shaped beaded design element on the cape of a two-hide dress that had replaced and originally symbolized the animal tail: "Over time somebody started the tradition that it symbolized a lake, and then a turtle." Seen in the dress on pp. 44, 45, the symbol of the turtle for the Sioux possessed power in the realm of women's health, including "conception, birth, and the period of the child's infancy."[25] During the mid 1800s, blue beads were favored to create fully beaded yokes in a fashion referred to as "blue breast beading." The blue beaded area represented "a lake or a body of water, in which the reflection of the blue sky can be seen. Small designs within this area of blue beadwork traditionally signify the reflections of those supernatural Beings who live in the sky or on the lake shore. Thus, stars are sometimes represented by a beaded design that originally was four-pointed.... Clouds are symbolized by double triangular designs."[26] Dresses with this style of beaded design, including the one seen on p. 47, were continually created from the 1850s to the 1870s.

The creativity of Native beadwork designs continues to this day. Joyce Growing Thunder Fogarty recalls visiting relatives who were consistently doing beadwork as she was growing up on the Fort Peck Indian Reservation: "I watched my grandmothers do a lot of beadwork on the reservation. Whenever we went to visit them, they were always beading. My grandmothers didn't have very big places to sit and bead, so they would just bead on their beds, having everything spread out. They didn't have designs to follow or anything. And that was amazing to me because of how they could do that—it just came out of their heads."

Sioux two-hide pattern
dress with fully beaded
yoke, ca. 1865. Probably
South Dakota. Deerhide,
seed beads, tin cones,
sinew. 5/958

From the 1870s on, yokes
completely covered in
beadwork became a
trademark of dresses
made by Sioux women.
To get a larger decorative
surface, women used
three hides, but still followed a two-hide pattern.

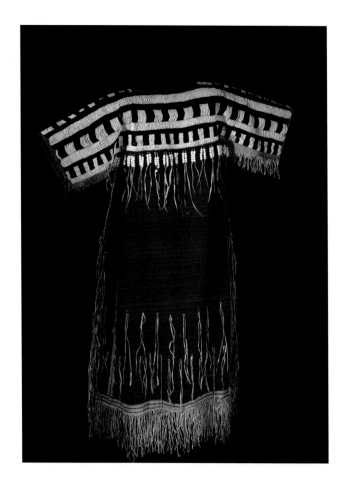

Joyce also speaks of the spiritual side of beadwork. Juanita Growing Thunder Fogarty comments that when her mother Joyce was beading and everything was going well, she would remark, "Oh, I must have had a lot of help on this one." Juanita explains that her mother understands that "there are spirits that come along with [beading]."

Creating a beaded dress is a time-consuming undertaking, and completing even one dress is a considerable accomplishment. Juanita says that it took her five years to make her first dress. Her mother would make her sit and bead instead of running around as young people like to do. "It's kind of a womanhood rite," Juanita explains. "When a Sioux girl finishes her first fully beaded top, she becomes a woman."

Sioux beadwork reached its highest elaboration from the late 1800s to the early 1900s. During confinement on reservations, dressmakers found time to create what came to be known as the "traditional Sioux style" of

Blackfoot cloth dress, ca. 1860. Canada. Striped saved-list red wool, blue wool, pony beads, glass trade beads, seed beads, thread. 4/4667

During a ten-year period—between 1850 and 1860—women were transitioning from pony beads to seed beads, which were smaller and easier to use. This dress includes both. The artist used cloth to make her dress, but added hide fringe to the yoke and hem.

Joyce Growing Thunder Fogarty (Assiniboine/Sioux) wearing a traditional Assiniboine-style dress that she made. Grass Valley, California, 1986.

Sicangu Lakota (Sioux)
two-hide pattern dress
with fully beaded yoke,
ca. 1870. South Dakota.
Hide, seed beads, sinew.
16/2493

Between 1850 and 1870,
Sioux artists began bead-
ing the background of the
yoke with blue beads. The
background represents a
lake, and the designs on
the yoke may be reflec-
tions of clouds or symbols
of the Four Directions.

dress (see p. 100). The motif of the American Flag was incorporated in the design of many beaded items, including the dress on pp. 48 and 151, for various reasons. Dances and sacred ceremonies such as the Sun Dance held annually in the summer were banned by the federal government. In their place, huge celebrations were held over the Fourth of July and other patriotic or Christian holidays. Women made elaborate dresses for these celebrations, turning the enforced idleness of confinement to their advantage by using the extra time to experiment with designs such as squared sleeves and American flags. Flags were seen as a token of friendship and given as gifts at treaty negotiations, conferring status on the receiver. In addition, the highly popular Wild West Shows of the time exposed Native people to patriotic flag designs.[27]

Today, beaded flag designs often symbolize a relative's service in the military. Juanita Growing Thunder Fogarty was taught by her mother that what was beaded on dresses would frequently "reflect what the people saw, and what they had going on in their lives at the time ... maybe somebody in their family had gone to war or battle."

The period of confinement on reservations was also a time of experimentation, and some dresses made during this time departed from the established style. The availability of a greater color selection of beads spurred the creation of more highly wrought designs. The yoke patterns were squared in some instances, losing the tapered shape of the animal leg (see p. 51).

Sioux two-hide pattern dress with fully beaded yoke decorated with American Flag motif (detail). See p. 151.

Arapaho two-hide pattern dress with fully beaded yoke, ca. 1900. Wyoming. Hide, seed beads, sinew. 9627

Opposite: Hunkpapa Lakota (Sioux) cloth dress, ca. 1910. North Dakota. Saved-list green wool, cowrie shells, ribbons, brass sequins, black cloth, thread. 23/2977

Cowrie shells and ribbons with flag patterns decorate this dress and suggest that the Lakota artist made it to be worn at a Fourth of July celebration.

Georgianna Old Elk (Assiniboine) says that the dress she wears to dance in was "gifted to her" by her extended family in Canada. Old Elk, whose Assiniboine name means "To Cry For Her" or "To Cry Over Her," says that the design of her dress tells a story that came to her in a dream:

> I'm gifted with eight eagle staffs on my dress, four in the front and four in back, because I come from a family of warriors—those who are serving now, those who have gone, and those who are yet to come. I have four lodges on my dress and four tipis (one is mine; the other three belong to my children—my son and two daughters). Pipes that cross the toes of my moccasins represent the fact that I am a pipe carrier. Green on the tips of my moccasins represents Mother Earth, which I highly respect. I also have Sun Dance colors [black, red, yellow, and white] in my dress because I am a Sun Dancer. I have a turtle on my back for longevity.

"I'm just the first keeper; it's not mine," says Old Elk of the dress that she hopes to pass on someday to daughter Dora or Anna or, eventually, to a future granddaughter. Wearing and dancing in her dress connects her with those relatives who created her dress: "When I dance I am never alone. Not only with my dress, but every bit of me or every part I wear was made by family. Even though they are gone now, they are still with me, and I feel them with me. So, I know I am never alone. I believe in the power of my dress and who made it for me."

Georgianna Old Elk (Assiniboine), 2006. Georgianna was recently honored by family members from Canada with a fully beaded yoke dress created especially for her. She danced in this dress at the NMAI National Pow-wow at the MCI (Verizon) Center in Washington, D.C., August 2005.

THREE-HIDE DRESSES

Today, many of the larger dance competitions draw people from both the Northern and Southern tribes of the Plains. The artistry of the women and their beaded dresses is something to marvel at. The novice observer may not be aware of the differences between the two groups; the Northern women, for instance, usually have fully beaded yokes whereas the Southern women have less beadwork on the dress. The beaded accessories, including crown, hair ties, belt, and belt accessories, make it clear, however, that dressmakers from both groups devote much talent and many long hours to their outfits.

The classic three-hide dress is made with one hide forming the poncho-like cape and one hide for the front and one for the back of the skirt. The legs of the hide are left intact on the dress. Keri Jhane Myers, a Comanche dressmaker and champion Southern Buckskin-style dance competitor, says that the hides are left in their natural shape: "We try to use everything in its natural form. When you folded a deerskin over to make the top for a three-hide dress, two legs would hang on each side of the dress" (see p. 55).

Southern-style dresses have the cape sewn to a skirt made from two hides, one each for front and back. Contemporary dresses are more likely to be made of commercially tanned hide because these hides are easily obtainable and the almost flawless, creamy white texture adds to the overall appearance of the dress. Five hides are used to create the contemporary Southern dress; two extra hides are needed just to make the long fringe attached to the cape. The dance style of the Southern women is a graceful walk, and once the dancer gets her fringe dancing, its mesmeric sway adds to the overall movement. "The fringes are long," Myers observes. "Probably within the past ten years, the fringes have really gained a lot of length. When our dancing happens, we have the fringes swinging back and forth in motion to the drum."

The three-hide dress has been adapted at other times in its history. In August 2006, I visited Kiowa artist and dressmaker Vanessa Jennings at her home near Anadarko, Oklahoma, and

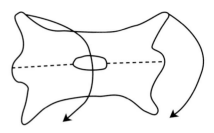
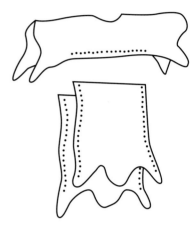

Diagram of a three-hide dress.

Dancers with their fringes in motion, NMAI National Powwow at the MCI (Verizon) Center in Washington, D.C., August 2005.

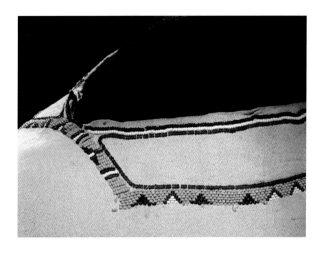

Kiowa three-hide dress, ca. 1880. Oklahoma. Black-tailed deerhide, brass spots, seed beads, sinew. 2/2172

In the Southern Plains, the three-hide dress consists of a cape attached to a skirt made from two hides. Historically, this style mimicked a poncho-and-skirt combination worn by women living as far south as Mexico.

Rebecca Brady, a former
Miss Indian Oklahoma and
a champion powwow
dancer, at the Schemitzun
Powwow in Connecticut,
2003. Her dress and accessories, created by Rebecca
and her husband Jon and
incorporating designs that
reflect their membership
in the Native American
Church, are pictured on
pp. 58–59.

discussed the construction of the Kiowa style three-hide dress with Vanessa
and her aunt, Dorothy White Horse. Dorothy told me that during World War
II, Kiowa women made dresses of white canvas because of the ration situation
and the fact that hides were unavailable. The dressmakers decorated the canvas dresses just as if they were decorating a hide dress. Dorothy said that the
beadwork and fringe traditionally used on the beautiful Kiowa buckskin dresses
also embellished the canvas dresses, and that everyone was doing their part for
the war effort.

Early Cheyenne-style three-hide dresses show the cape attached to the skirt
section and decorated with three beaded strips. Historic photographs show
that the practice of decorating the cape with three beaded strips was shared
with the Comanche. Three beaded strips, however, have remained characteristic of a Cheyenne-style dress (see p. 56).

Rebecca Brady and her husband Jon created a three-hide dress in a Cheyenne
style. Although Rebecca is enrolled in the Sac and Fox tribes, she is also de-
scended from the Cheyenne. According to Rebecca, the three beaded strips on
the cape are what make her dress Cheyenne (see below, left and p. 58). The

Bradys are members of the Native American
Church, which blends Christian and Native beliefs, and their faith in this church inspired the
creation of her dress. The beadwork designs
symbolize several elements of the Church: the
tipi represents the ritual or meeting, which is
held at night, the beaded green cactus represents
Grandfather Peyote, and the birdlike design represents the water bird (Anhanga), which carries
prayers to God.

Rebecca and Jon Brady created a second set
of beadwork for their daughter Cheyenne (see
pp. 60, 61). Additional symbols representative
of the Native American Church are depicted in
the beadwork, including a water drum formed
from a three-legged iron kettle filled with water
and topped with a hide cover. The three legs of
the kettle represent the Trinity (Father, Son, and
Holy Ghost). The tone of the drum changes as
it is played because the water moves about within

Cheyenne three-hide dress and accessories, ca. 1995. Made by Rebecca Brady (Cheyenne/Sac and Fox, b. 1969) and Jon Brady (Arikara, b. 1976). Oklahoma. Commercial hide, cut glass beads, rainbow selvage white wool, ribbons, cowrie shells, hairpipes, fire-polished glass beads, rhinestones, horse-hair, cotton, paint, canvas, rawhide, thread. 26/5186

the kettle. The drum is used when singing prayer songs during the night meeting. Three fans with feathers of flickers, eagles, and macaws—used to send prayers to God—are also represented in the beadwork designs, as are rattles used in Native American Church ceremony.

WOOL AND COTTON DRESSES

Wool cloth produced in England was a favored trade item. As I mentioned earlier in this essay, the cloth, made in lengths of fifty-four inches, was dyed with a white edge called "saved-list" that Native dressmakers incorporated into their dress pattern. The T-shaped dress pattern utilized the length of the material, and the side panels, or gussets, were reminiscent of the deer legs on hide dresses. The cloth came in colors of blue, scarlet, green, and yellow. Blue and scarlet were colors highly desired by the Sioux, Cheyenne, and Arapaho, as well as the Kiowa (see p. 26). Green cloth was admired among the Crow. Wool dresses were decorated with cowrie and dentalium shells, ribbons, and brass sequins, among other items (see pp. 50, 116). Dresses made of cloth were fashionable in earlier days because of the material's rarity, but once trade cloth became more

Above left: Cheyenne Brady at the 2001 Denver March Powwow in Colorado, wearing a dress and accessories made for her by her parents Rebecca and Jon Brady. Opposite: Another cloth dress created for her by her parents was given to the NMAI.

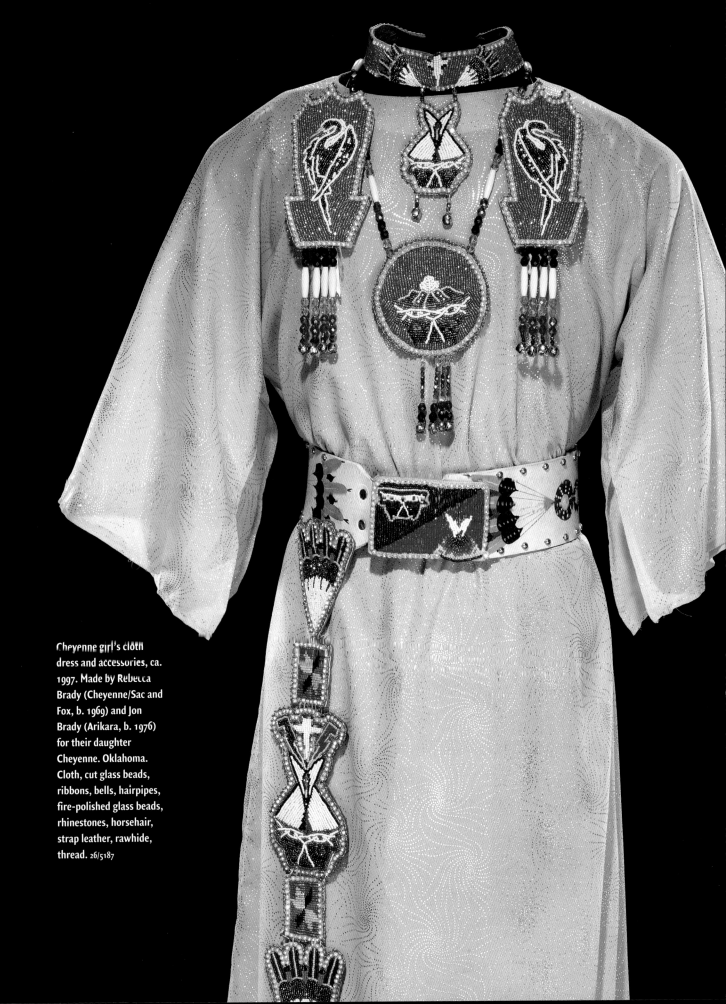

Cheyenne girl's cloth
dress and accessories, ca.
1997. Made by Rebecca
Brady (Cheyenne/Sac and
Fox, b. 1969) and Jon
Brady (Arikara, b. 1976)
for their daughter
Cheyenne. Oklahoma.
Cloth, cut glass beads,
ribbons, bells, hairpipes,
fire-polished glass beads,
rhinestones, horsehair,
strap leather, rawhide,
thread. 26/5187

available, dresses of hide came back in vogue, particularly among the Kiowa.

Broadcloth, a lighter-weight cotton cloth, was introduced by fur traders and store merchants as a trade item and was also used for treaty payments. Broadcloth was used to make everyday cotton dresses. In colder weather, several layers of dresses were often worn. Since broadcloth dresses were daily attire, they are rarely found in museum collections. Contemporary dresses are made from calico, wool, satin, and other materials and worn for every occasion from powwows to graduations to religious ceremonies such as Sun Dances.

CONCLUSION

Each dress holds a story. Most dresses in museum collections have documentation about who collected the dress but little is known about who made the dress. Rarely do we know much about the rich spirit and thought involved in its creation. With living dressmakers, we are fortunate to be able to gain insight into this process. Listen, for example, to the words of Juanita Growing Thunder Fogarty: "A lot of dresses have sound. I have coins on my dress. I like it when I can hear the clinking of my coins or the snapping of my fringes when I'm dancing. It's all a part of the feeling that the dress is alive." And Jackie Parsons, our dress designer and artist from the Blackfeet Nation of Montana, encompasses much as she says, "When I'm wearing a Blackfeet dress that I have made, I feel really powerful, because I feel so very connected to everything around me."

The beautiful dresses in *Identity by Design*—made by women from Native nations on both sides of the U.S.-Canada border—reveal the artistic talent and individuality of their creators as well as different regional styles and tribal designs. Ranging in time from the 1830s to the present day, they serve to illuminate Native history and identity during a time of intense social and cultural change. For contemporary women artists, dresses are more than garments. They are evidence of a proud and unbroken tradition, links to the generations of women who came before them, and bridges to the future.

NOTES

1. N. Scott Momaday, *The Way to Rainy Mountain* (Albuquerque: University of New Mexico Press, 1969), 82.

2. Norman Feder, "The Side Fold Dress," *American Indian Art Magazine* 10, no.1 (Winter 1984): 48.

3. Interview conducted at the National Pow-wow held by NMAI in August of 2005. Unless otherwise noted, all quotations from contemporary artists in this essay derive from interviews conducted with the artists by Emil Her Many Horses and Colleen Cutschall at NMAI's National Powwow in Washington, D.C., August 2005, and at NMAI in December 2005.

4. Feder, "The Side Fold Dress," 50.

5. Ibid., 51.

6. Quoted in Colin F. Taylor (translation into German, Wolfgang Neuhaus), *Yupika: The Plains Indian Woman's Dress; An Overview of Historical Developments and Styles/Die Kleidung der Plainsindianer-Frauen; Ein Überblick über historische Entwicklungen und Stile* (Wyk auf Foehr: Verlag für Amerikanistik, 2003), 26.

7. Castle McLaughlin, *Arts of Diplomacy: Lewis and Clark's Indian Collection* (Seattle: University of Washington Press, 2003), 82.

8. Colin F. Taylor, *The Plains Indians: A Cultural and Historical View of the North American Plains Tribes of the Pre-Reservation Period* (London: Salamander Books, 1994), 125.

9. Evan Maclyn Maurer, *The Native American Heritage: A Survey of North American Indian Art* (The Art Institute of Chicago, 1977), 40.

10. Lois Sherr Dubin, *The History of Beads: From 30,000 B.C. to the Present* (New York: Harry N. Abrams, 1987), 274.

11. McLaughlin, 82.

12. Taylor, *The Plains Indians*, 130.

13. Ibid.

14. Maurer, 40.

15. McLaughlin, 38.

16. Dubin, 274.

17. Susan Jennys, *19th Century Plains Indian Dresses* (Pottsboro, TX: Crazy Crow Trading Post, 2005), 21.

18. Taylor, *The Plains Indians,* 130.

19. Richard Conn, *A Classification of Aboriginal North American Clothing* (Seattle: University of Washington Press, 1955), 33.

20. Lillian Ackerman, ed., *A Song to the Creator: Traditional Arts of Native American Women of the Plateau* (Norman: University of Oklahoma Press, 1996), 112.

21. Dubin, 274.

22. Jennys, 62.

23. Ibid., 10.

24. Ibid., 22.

25. Clark Wissler, *Decorative Art of the Sioux Indians* [Bulletin of the American Museum of Natural History 18, no. 3] (New York: American Museum of Natural History, 1904), 242.

26. Maurer, 45.

27. Tony Herbst and Joel Kopp, *The Flag in American Indian Art* (Seattle: University of Washington Press, 1993), 17–19.

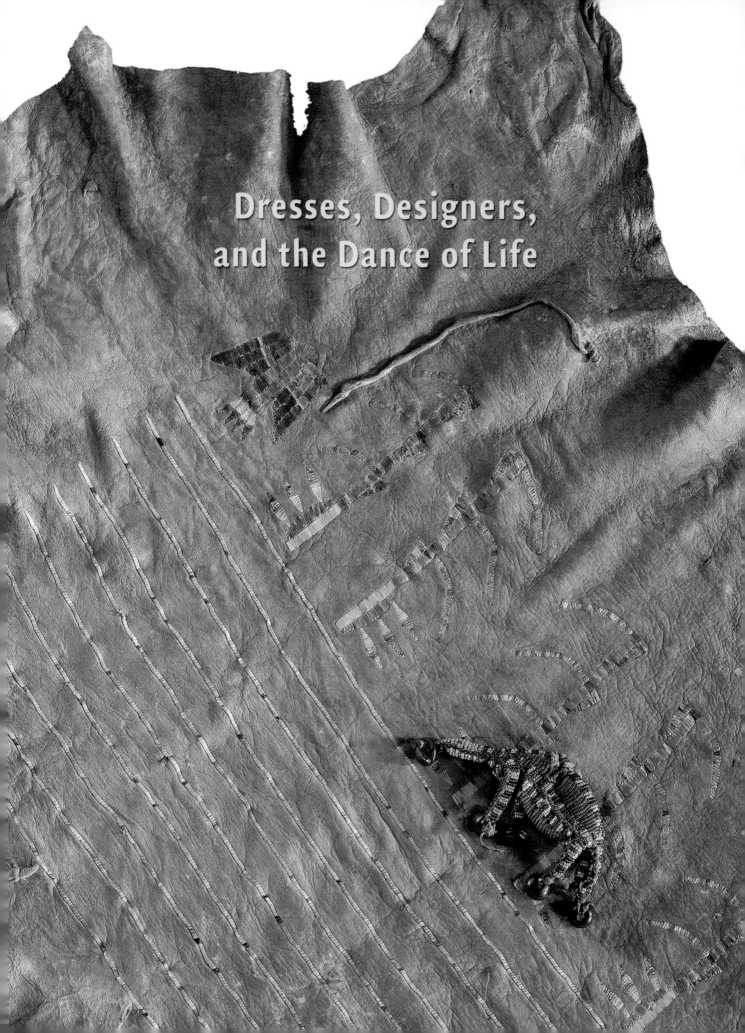

Dresses, Designers,
and the Dance of Life

IN THE BADLANDS OF THE NORTHERN PLAINS, a cooking bag begins to boil. A grandmother sets aside a large buffalo robe and slowly gets up to tend her soup. As she stirs the sparse liquid and stokes the fire, her only companion, a dog, makes his way to her buffalo robe unseen. He paws at the newly sewn porcupine quills on the robe, undoing the design the old woman has just completed. As she returns to sit at her work, she sees that it has been undone. The dog shies away from her, perhaps sensing that he may soon be added to the soup. In Lakota oral tradition, this action is repeated over and over again. It is said that if the grandmother ever completes the quilled robe, then the world will end.

The grandmother is an enduring symbol of indigenous women's artistic abilities and of their labor. A sort of "Grandmother Time," she represents the women of many generations who sew, quill, bead, or paint for themselves and their relatives, and thus bring beauty into all their lives. The relationship of these creators to the natural world is evident through their choice of materials. The spirit, bones, sinews, teeth, and hides of animals such as deer, elk, and buffalo and quills of the porcupine are combined to create striking attire. Other nations of the natural world are also called upon as needed. The winged and water creatures provide feathers, shells, claws, and small bones to adorn clothing. The personalities of the women and the animal nations combine in unique ways to communicate both message and beauty.

Sioux robe (detail).
See p. 68.

Identity by Design: Tradition, Change, and Celebration in Native Women's Dresses brings together dresses from the Plains, Plateau, and Great Basin regions, juxtaposing the fashion gifts of the grandmothers with the voices of the granddaughters and great-granddaughters, who themselves carry on the art of making dresses and designing accessories. These women dress themselves, their families, and their communities to partake in the dance of life. The memories, wisdom, and experience of contemporary Native women artists whose many skills include dressmaking explain how the past resonates in the present and what is being done to ensure that future generations continue traditions that reinforce tribal identity. With the help of their voices, I examine here the ongoing spiritual and symbolic roles of women during the significant stages of life and how clothing helps to form and express their identities and worldviews.

As the daughter of Lakota fashion designer Geraldine Sherman, I grew up watching my mother select patterns, fabrics, ribbons, trims, and buttons and observing the layout of garments in various stages of preparation, sewing, and finishing. The fabric textures and color arrangements were always the most mesmerizing and pleasing to me, and somehow made up for the hours of assuming the role of human pincushion while being measured and poked (and inevitably becoming the victim of a straight pin left in a finished garment). I was al-

Two Sioux girls, ca. 1890. Probably South Dakota or North Dakota. Photo by Fred E. Miller. N13650

Sioux robe (detail). See p. 68.

ways amazed at my mother's dedication to producing fashions hour after hour, day after day, working at the sewing machine. She never seemed to tire and was always talking about the next piece she would make. Her artistic fortitude and persistence—and that of grandmothers I never met—motivated me as an artist to develop a hatched painting technique that resembles the textures produced through quill- and beadwork. Later, I learned to prepare and tan hides and produce tipi doors and liners. Today, as in the past, early training of a dressmaker/designer often begins in the formative years in the home with female relatives as guides and mentors.

WALKING IN BEAUTY

Women's accomplishments continue to be lavished on relatives, especially children. From infancy, children are exposed to tribal values and aesthetics through participation in public display and performance arts focused on dance and ritual. Gladys Jefferson, who lives on the Crow Reservation in Montana and is active in preserving traditional culture, including beadwork and dressmaking, explains:

> As part of the naming ceremony, the person who gives a child her Crow name wraps the child's umbilical cord and makes prayers with it. The name-giver beads the covering and returns it to the girl when she starts walking. This object might be worn attached to one's back or tied to the end of a scarf.... The Crow love their children and their grandchildren. They want to show them off, so even before children are walking, parents and grandparents outfit them and bring them to dances. A little girl's first dress is passed on. Then as she grows and has personal achievements, her relatives make her a dress.[1]

Among the Lakota, orphans and those who have lost relatives may be formally adopted by a member of the community and supported and guided through life. The young girls in the photograph on p. 66 have their faces painted, indicating that they have just been adopted in the Hunka (Making of Relatives) Ceremony. Throughout their lives, they will have the right to wear their face paint on ceremonial occasions. The porcupine quilled robe on p. 68, decorated with Hunka staffs that appear above the rows of quillwork and are flanked by eagles, would have been worn by a child who had gone through this ceremony. The robe is in a style called Road of Life, in which the rows of quillwork represent the many paths one takes in life. The beaded turtle amulet attached to the robe contains the child's umbilical cord.

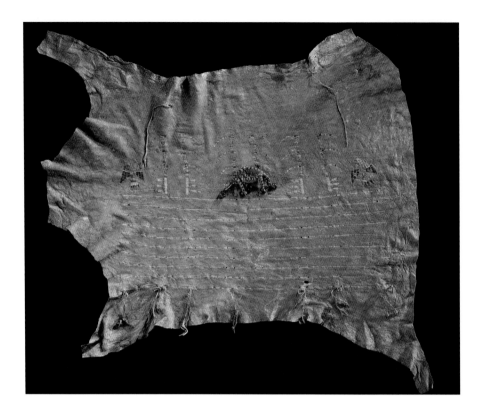

Sioux robe, ca. 1880. South Dakota. Hide, porcupine quills, seed beads, brass bells, sinew. 2195

Through public displays and rituals, a young girl's identity takes shape. Noted traditional Southern Buckskin dancer Keri Jhane Myers (Comanche) is also a dressmaker who creates clothing and accessories that she wears in competition. Myers, pictured on pp. 80 and 91, talks about the significance of clothing to one's sense of self:

> As a young child, you don't have the right to wear eagle feathers or eagle plumes until you have proven yourself to your family. I'm an elder's child, and I was the first grandchild. In our Comanche culture, the first grandchild is usually raised by the grandparents. And that's where you learn how to craft. So at an early age, I learned to bead. I learned to cut buckskin and make the things that were representative of my family. Young girls wearing crowns on public occasions do not all have a feather plume. A plumeless crown means that the girl has not yet received her name. At her naming, around the age of eight or nine, a girl receives a single eagle feather plume that she wears the rest of her life with her dress. She also receives face paint on her ears. In addition, a firstborn child is marked with a single line from eye to ear. These markings provide spiritual protection to those named and identify them to other tribal members.

Omaha woman tattooed with Mark of Honor. This glass negative image appeared in the *Twenty-Seventh Annual Report of the Bureau of American Ethnology to the Secretary of the Smithsonian Institution, 1905–1906.*

THREADS OF WOMANHOOD

When girls reached adolescence, they went though elaborate ceremonies to prepare for womanhood, marriage, and family. Wearing dresses created by their families specifically for this passage, girls were able to identify more fully with their new responsibilities and gain confidence in their skills and artistry. Girls and their families eagerly anticipated and planned for the events that marked this time of life. People of the Plains, Plateau, and Great Basin regarded a girl on the threshold of womanhood as one of the most potent agents of life-renewing powers, capable of bringing blessings to the entire community. Unfortunately, in the last century many of the rites, songs, and meanings related to ceremonies attending this time of life have been lost. Previously, in these charged moments of spiritual significance, the newly pubescent girl would be aligned to the movements of the cosmos and her life path. Through her initiation ceremony, she is transformed into a living world axis. She becomes the sacred center, connecting her people to the spirit world above and below.

Among the Omaha, certain young women whose fathers belonged to the Hon'hewachi Society were distinguished by receiving the Mark of Honor, cosmic symbols ceremonially tattooed on forehead and throat (see above). Alice Fletcher and Francis La Flesche, who recorded Omaha life in the late nineteenth century, wrote that a young woman thus tattooed was called a "woman chief," and that she received the Mark of Honor on a bed of fine robes, facing west "for, being emblematic of life, she had to lie as if moving with the sun." [2] The tattooing was completed as the sun passed directly overhead; as anthropologist Robin Ridington observed:

> The mark on the young woman's forehead symbolized the sun at its zenith, "from which point it speaks," and its lifegiving power passes through her body and out into the camp circle. The mark on her throat was a four-pointed star radiating out from a perfect circle.... The young woman received the sun's power when she was at a point on the earth's surface directly between the earth's center and the highest point in the sun's heavenly arc.... She found herself centered between earth and sky.[3]

Through ceremony, a young woman can become a living representative of revered spirit beings such as Changing Woman of the Apache and White Buffalo Calf Woman of the Lakota who were known to have brought the arts, sacred corn, beauty, compassion, healing, truth, and ethics to the people through teachings and rituals.

Changing Woman, the spirit being also called White Shell Woman because she came ashore in a shell, brought the arts of basketry, sewing, and ceremony to the Apache. Her presence infuses the Apache Sunrise Ceremony that marks a young girl's entry into womanhood. In this ritual, a group of ceremonially dressed (see the outfit on p. 71) and painted young Apache girls dance, kneel, and lie on buckskin. Thirty-two songs of beauty and goodness are imparted to them. The girls make runs between the buckskin and a ceremonial basket; these symbolize the different life stages of childhood, girlhood, womanhood, and old age. They also run to the four directions. The runs encourage good character by reinforcing the four life objectives of physical strength, a fine disposition, prosperity, and a healthy old age. On the final day, the singers face the dawning sun and bless the girls with corn pollen. Saturated in the sacred, the girls can bring blessings and healing to themselves and those around them.

National Museum of the American Indian staff member Pamela Woodis (Jicarilla Apache), whose family has a long tradition of making dresses and accessories, describes the Keesda Ceremony of the Jicarilla Apache and the special role of the dress worn for this occasion:

> The Apache mother and grandmother make a dress for the Keesda Ceremony. That dress is never danced publicly at powwows or any social dances. It can be worn more than once, but only for puberty dances or puberty ceremonies—you could hand it down to your daughters. The buckskin dress has minimal beading, limited to the edge of the cape around the neck and down the shoulders. It is worn with a bone necklace and a shell to represent White Shell Woman. Specific songs for each part of the outfit meld the girl's spirit with that of the dress. Her face is painted with yellow ochre in powder form as a blessing or for protection. Yellow paint is also used on dresses to beautify and signify a tribe or tribal identity. On the last day, after the last songs are done, the girl puts aside her puberty dress and her ceremonial role of White Shell Woman. Her purification is complete as her face is painted with red ochre, and she steps into womanhood. The same red ochre paint powder, which brings a blessing, is used to paint the faces of her family and all the people present at the ceremony.

White Mountain Apache girl's cape and skirt, ca. 1905. Arizona. Hide, yellow paint, tin cones, German silver spots, sinew. 9/4065 and 9/4064

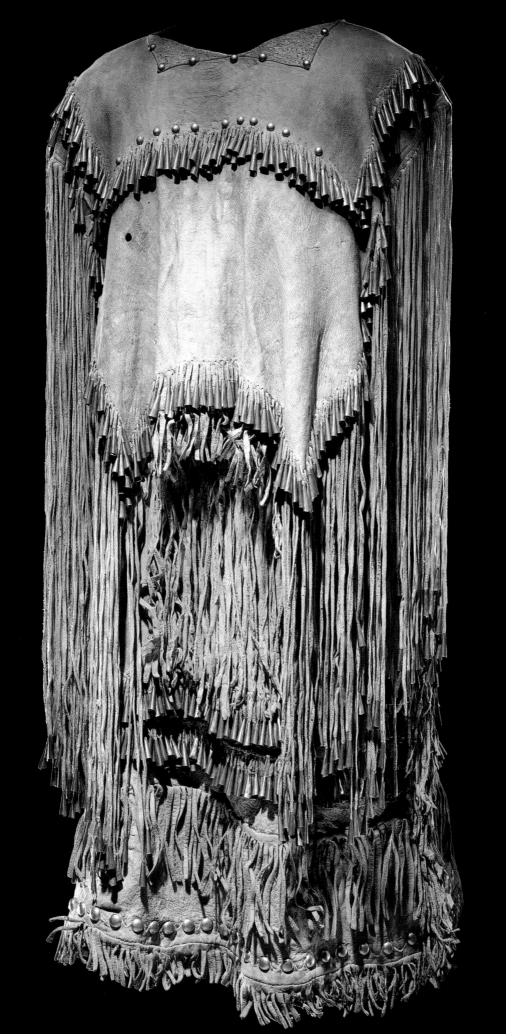

Colleen Cutschall (Oglala Lakota, b. 1951), *The Pregnant Grandfather*, 1988. Acrylic on canvas, 121.9 x 121.9 cm. Collection of the Manitoba Arts Council, Canada.

This painting represents an origin story about the female spirit being Maka, who, in the avatar of the Pregnant Grandfather, participates in the council of all the great beings. Maka is responsible for the plants and animals. The image, which links Maka, the earth, and the female principle, can also be viewed as the beaded yoke of a woman's dress.

The experience of ceremony is greatly enriched by the knowledge of our original instructions given in creation stories. Many of my own paintings and installation works have been inspired by creation stories. The series *Voice in the Blood*, first exhibited in 1990, depicts Lakota creation stories through large paintings that interpret the creation of the great spirit beings; the cosmos, plants, and animals; the emergence of the Lakota; and the establishment of shamanic traditions. The image in one painting can be viewed as the beaded yoke of a woman's dress that symbolizes a lake, out of which living things grow (see p. 72). This series was the culmination of several years of intense ritual practice involving sweat lodges, vision questing, Sun Dancing, and sponsoring naming ceremonies or assisting other initiates in their practice. Through ritual and public ceremony, our creation stories are reenacted.

White Buffalo Calf Woman, also known as Wohpe and Falling Star, brought the Lakota their most sacred relic, a pipe. Daughter of the great sky spirit, she carries all prayers between humans and the spirit being that is called upon. In the ancient creation, she mediated between the other great beings and helped bring about order in the cosmos. Through the pipe, she mediates between the Lakota and their ancient grandparents. She was responsible for refining the great ceremony of the Sun Dance.

At Sun Dances, I have observed young virgin girls chosen to represent the White Buffalo Calf Woman and preside over the several-day ritual. These mundane and often immature teenagers are transformed into calm, compassionate, and understanding young women. This world renewal ceremony is initiated when a young woman walks into the Sun Dance lodge and presents the sacred pipe to the chiefs. The pipe is law, and whatever one promises in dance or speech with the pipe is absolutely contracted with the Creator. By the sacred cottonwood tree that stands in the ceremonial center, female initiates and supplicants, such as the little girls chosen to make ritual chops at the tree (known as "tree choppers"), will have their ears pierced—as my daughter did when she was five years old—or sing for women who give flesh offerings from their upper arms as I have done at Sun Dances. Blood is the most important offering and the central element for renewal.

Clothing for high ceremony today is the opposite of elaborate formal fashion for public secular events. It is characterized by plainness. Although the dress worn for a Sun Dance is usually new, it lacks ornamentation and is worn without moccasins or leggings. The woman stands alone, unadorned before her Creator. She might wear a simple cotton dress like the underdresses usually

RECEIVING INSTRUCTIONS DURING SUN DANCE - ROSEBUD, S.D.   ONEILL PHOTO CO.

worn beneath heavier wool dresses (see p. 75). As indicated in a photograph of male and female Sun Dancers (see above), women did occasionally wear their formal fashions. The absence of such attire today indicates both a diminution of traditional dressmaking and recognition that the ritual is more important than formal dress requirements.

For a 1992 exhibition entitled *Cloister*, I created an installation called *Sisterwolf in Her Moon* to represent a Native woman's period of seclusion during her menses. Such moon-time practices were once found throughout the Plains, Plateau, and Great Basin. Lakota women traditionally began their formal training as artists and designers with the commencement of their menses. This training was intrinsically tied to a girl's biological, emotional, psychological, and spiritual growth into womanhood. During the Ishna Ta Awi Cha Lowan, the preparing for womanhood ceremony among the Lakota, a girl experiencing her first menstrual cycle was secluded from the community, from hunting trails, and, in particular, from males. The ceremony is literally translated as "Her Alone They Sing Over." She was expected to complete a pair of quilled or beaded moccasins during her solitude. To symbolize her transformed state of being at the conclusion of the ceremony, a young woman's clothes were burned, and she received a new set.

Sicangu Lakota men and women receiving instructions during the Sun Dance, ca. 1910. Rosebud Reservation, South Dakota. Photo by O'Neill Photo Company. P22346

Arapaho cloth dress, ca. 1890. Wyoming. Purple cloth, thread. 20/5940

Cloth was often distributed by the U.S. government as part of treaty allotments. The Arapaho artist who made this everyday dress may have received the cloth that way. This dress would have been worn with a belt and shawl, and in the colder months, a woman would layer several of these dresses over one another for warmth.

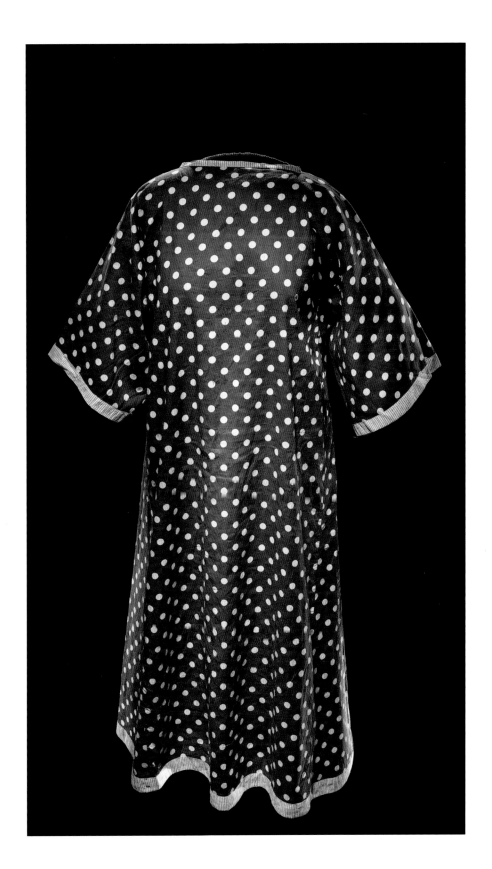

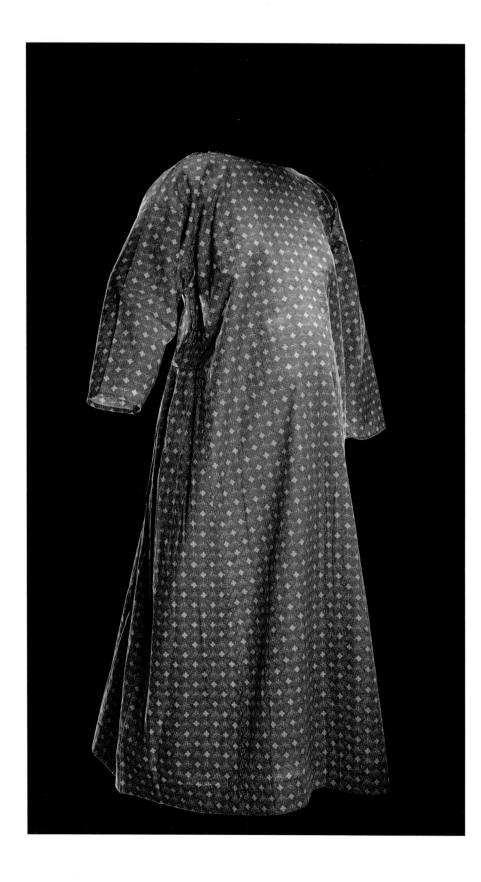

Mandan cloth dress, ca. 1880. North Dakota. Cloth, thread. 19/628

Made of cotton cloth bought from a trader or store merchant, this dress is loose-fitting and the pleats allow it to expand.

A Cheyenne woman using a smoother on a finished piece of quillwork, ca. 1902. Lame Deer, Montana. Photo by Elizabeth Grinnell. N13620

Yankton Sioux beaded awl case, ca. 1880. Quill-wrapped fringe, tin cones, and yarn. 17/9737

In 1904, anthropologist Clark Wissler wrote about turtle symbolism in designs on Native women's dresses, asserting, "this had power over the functional diseases peculiar to women."[4] Until the latter twentieth century such references to women's natural processes as illness did much to undermine the dignity of women and create a perception of them as impaired. This lack of understanding that Native women's blood is at the core of their spiritual potency also promoted a negative interpretation of the cultural rules pertaining to women in relation to ceremonies and the handling of sacred objects.

Women are seen as being in opposition to spiritually renewing energies at a time when they themselves were physically going through a miniaturized death. Each month, the unappropriated life within the woman's body is dispelled while simultaneously purifying the body

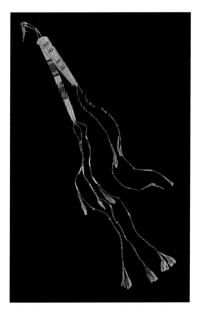

and preparing it to receive new life. Each time this occurs, the woman is in a highly potent spiritual state that is considered dangerous. The Lakota acknowledge this special state by referring to her as a holy and mysterious woman.

SOCIETY WOMEN

As an adult, a woman had the responsibility of maintaining the home, which included providing clothing for her family and herself. Industriousness in women was valued, particularly the ability to sew, quill, and bead objects of excellence. Aesthetic skill was esteemed and on the Plains was supported through quilling societies. As Mourning Dove (Okanogan, 1888–1936) observed:

Crow woman and baby, ca. 1900. Montana. Photographer unknown. P09352

Flathead cradleboard, ca. 1880. Montana. Hide, seed beads, glass oval beads, shells, German silver spots, harness leather, wood, sinew. 14/3521

Considered gifts from the Creator, infants were carried in cradleboards for up to one year. The construction, beading technique, designs, and colors on each of these cradleboards are meant to physically and spiritually protect a child.

Keri Jhane Myers
(Comanche), 2005.

I use the heart design because it is contemporary. I have four children, and each is represented by a heart. I travel a lot—sometimes I am with my children and sometimes away from them. My oldest daughter is in college. So the design keeps my family with me and reminds me of my children, no matter where I go.

A very artistic designer made beautiful clothing decorated in many shades. Decoration was highly prized on adults' clothing, children's gear, and a baby's cradleboard. A wife with a decorative knack was much regarded by the community and brought fame to her husband and family. Such finery was not used daily, but only for occasions such as council meetings, social get-togethers accompanied by gambling, feasting or games, and religious gatherings.[5]

Lantern slide image of a Blackfeet woman, ca. 1890. Montana. Photographer unknown. L01219

This Blackfeet woman wears a wool dress decorated with basket beads, cowrie shells, and metal thimbles attached to fringes.

Women were inspired to create dresses that showed the scope of their creativity and evidence of their beliefs. Such inspiration continues today. Keri Jhane Myers incorporated a design featuring four hearts into her ensemble (see p. 80): "I use the heart design because it is contemporary. I have four children, and each is represented by a heart. I travel a lot—sometimes I am with my children and sometimes away from them. My oldest daughter is in college. So the design keeps my family with me and reminds me of my children, no matter where I go."

Connecting with her people through the elements used to decorate her dress is also vital to Myers. "For me, it's important when I travel away from my home that people know my tribal identity.... Comanches like to use the color blue, so I have a lot of blue in there [beadwork] ... and the Comanches used yellow to paint their dresses." Adding yellow-dyed horsehair to her dress is important to her because "the Comanches were the first Indians to have horses, which added a lot to our mobility and our trade."

Women participated in artistic, religious, and military societies that played active roles in preserving culture, often through dance. Women's societies had responsibility for medicine bundles and were charged with the authority of leading or initiating certain high ceremonies. Women were also participants in societies that performed annual agricultural rites

Regalia for the Crow Tobacco Society included dresses, leggings, and moccasins, as well as a pouch for medicine. The society performed annual tobacco planting and harvesting rites. Gladys Jefferson, a member of the Tobacco Society, describes the importance of tobacco to the Crow people:

> When the Crow and the Hidatsa were split up a long time ago, the Hidatsa were given the corn. Their brothers, the Crow, were given the tobacco plant and went to the Big Horn Mountains to place it in the ground. The Tobacco Society of the Crow represents our whole being. As long as we have the tobacco, we will always be here.

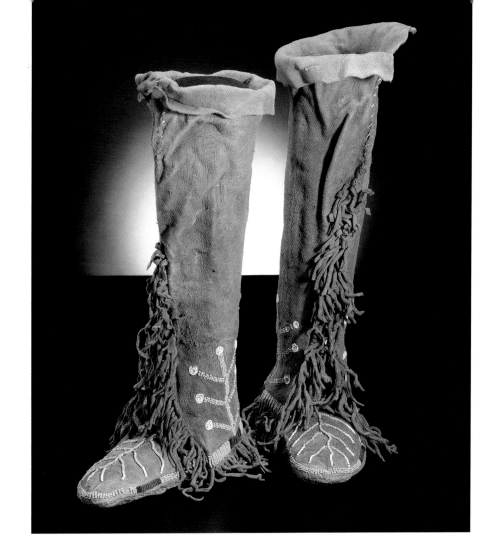

Crow Tobacco Society dress, ca. 1890. Montana. Muslin, medicine pouches, pony beads, red wool, red paint, ermine skins, thread. Shown with permission. 12/3098

Crow Tobacco Society moccasins, ca. 1890. Montana. Painted and beaded animal hide. Shown with permission. 12/3112

We offer tobacco all the time. Many things go along with the Tobacco Society. Membership is through adoption that entails an enormous exchange of gifts between the initiate's family and the sponsoring family. Members have tobacco dresses and pouches that they keep with their medicine bundles. If women in the house are on their menstrual period, the bundle must be taken out of the house or stored. Bundles are only taken to daytime Tobacco Dances. They must be put away before the sun goes down.

Tobacco Society moccasins are beaded with a root pattern. The leggings display the motif of a blossoming tobacco plant. With the meeting of moccasin and legging, the entire tobacco plant is represented as springing forth from the earth where the woman has planted the seeds (see above). Bracketed by sacred planting and harvesting rites performed by women who embody fertility and life, the growth of the tobacco plant ensures the health and success of the Crow people. Gladys says of the Tobacco Society garment pictured on p. 82:

Blackfeet dress, ca. 1900. Probably Montana. Red wool, ribbon, calico, fire-polished glass beads, pony beads, basket beads, metal thimbles, thread. 26/5470

Blackfoot bonnet, ca. 1890. Canada. Eagle tail feathers and plume, rooster hackle feathers, ermine skins, brass buttons, red wool, horsehair, rawhide, sinew. 22/7371

A Blackfeet woman wear-
ing an upright feather
bonnet, ca. 1900. Mon-
tana. Photo by the Camera
Art Company, St. Paul,
Minnesota. P20695

The dress is a sacred, ceremonial
type. We don't have these anymore.
Only about two or three of them remain. This particular dress is what
you wear when you're planting.
Not just anybody can plant tobacco—you have to have the right.
The women who do the planting
wear this kind of dress and have
their face and hands painted with
red ochre.

The purpose of women's societies
and dances varies—they occasionally
spring up in response to a perceived
societal need. Societies inevitably
adopt a fashion uniform that identi-
fies them within the community.
Jackie Parsons, Blackfeet dressmaker
and designer, talks about how these
societies evolved among her people:

A society is a group of people that
belong to a specific medicine bundle. The societies are all there to
help the people in specific ways.
Blackfeet women did not dance
until about the 1920s. The men al-
lowed the women to dance, but they could only dance with the men in a circle to the
Owl Dance. This dance was primarily a social dance and continues to the present
day. The women wanted to start their own dance, so they began their own society
called the Headdress Society (also called the War Bonnet Society) in which they did
the round dance. They all wore upright bonnets borrowed from their husbands. Big-
brimmed black felt hats with rounded stovepipe tops later replaced the bonnets. The
women used bells and thimbles to ornament dresses that were exclusive to their society. During World War II, the women started another society called the War Mothers Society. Now they're reviving that society because of Iraq.

SEWING SURVIVAL

Women became more actively involved in political and ceremonial affairs in the late nineteenth century as extreme governmental constraints on indigenous people developed. As the rarely seen Ghost Dance dress above and on p. 87 demonstrates, dress design responded to aspects of cultural opposition. Such dresses, boldly decorated with paint, emerged in the late 1880s as part of the rapidly spreading Ghost Dance movement led by a Paiute man named Wovoka. The December 1890 massacre of Lakota men, women, and children by U.S. soldiers at Wounded Knee in South Dakota effectively ended the visionary Ghost Dance. The dresses are seldom presented because of the tragic circumstances in which they were created and worn.

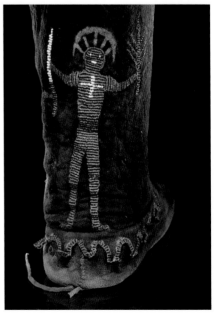

Arapaho Ghost Dance dress, ca. 1890. Probably Wyoming or Oklahoma. Hide, red, blue, green, and yellow paint, cloth, sinew. 2/8374; Arapaho Ghost Dance moccasins, ca. 1890. Probably Wyoming or Oklahoma. Hide, seed beads, blue paint, rawhide, sinew. Shown with permission. 12/878

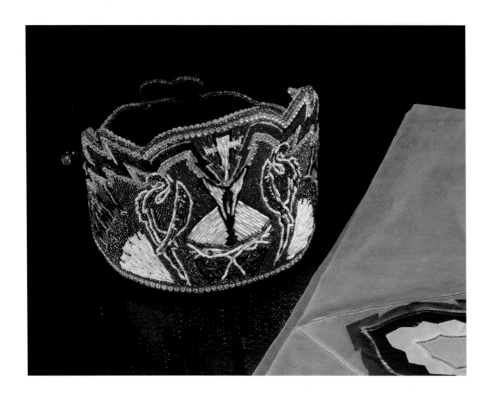

Crown and detail of shawl, among the accessories made by Rebecca Brady (Cheyenne/Sac and Fox, b. 1969) and Jon Brady (Arikara, b. 1976) for their daughter Cheyenne, ca. 1997. 26/5187

Purse and detail of shawl worn by Rebecca Brady (Cheyenne/Sac and Fox, b. 1969), made by Rebecca and her husband Jon Brady (Arikara, b. 1976), ca. 1995. 26/5186

The adoption of new rituals into well-established belief and ceremonial practices inspired innovative designs in dress ornamentation. Both buckskin and cloth Ghost Dance dresses were painted with highly charged symbols of nature and the elements and emblems of feminine identity. Thunderbird and new moon symbols frequently appear and speak to a hoped-for reversal of desperate conditions and the beginning of a new life. It would be foolish to assume that the stars and red and blue paint of the Arapaho dress on p. 87 indicated patriotic feelings for the United States at a time when many U.S. citizens considered Indians to be subhuman. Adherence to tribe and cultural belief are embodied in an image of a woman who, dressed in red, holds the sacred pipe in one hand and a branch of the holy cedar tree in the other. This portrait image wears and is flanked by the symbol of the morning star in both daytime and nighttime aspects. A similar figure of a male can be found on the high-top moccasins (see p. 86). A turtle, symbolizing protection of women and long life, is depicted on the lower part of the dress.

Native nations were losing the resources and land that had once sustained them, and their way of life was rapidly changing. Through painted signs of power, the universe was being called upon to rescue them from cultural genocide. When this new movement was unable to fulfill the promise of restored land, animals, and deceased relatives, it dissolved. Dressmakers returned to time-honored quill and bead decoration. The short-lived explosion of new painted dress designs ended, never to be revived. Other dress styles at any stage of their evolution belong to the cumulative corpus of indigenous garments. The fashion silence accorded Ghost Dance dresses has been said by Juanita Growing Thunder Fogarty (Assiniboine/Sioux) to be "out of respect to those dressmakers who were lost" and the families who endured the end of the Plains wars. The hush acknowledges a culturally tragic moment of historical transition.

New spiritual movements continued to be a rich source of decorative, symbolic expression on dresses. Chief Quanah Parker introduced the use of peyote—brought back to the Comanche from Mexico—for healing, and the practice spread throughout the Southern Plains and into the Northern Plains and Plateau country. The sacred peyote button, the peyote lodge, the waterbird, yellowhammers, the colors of early dawn, and other symbols associated with peyote are often found in the bead decoration of women's Southern-style outfits, as can be seen in the accessories pictured on p. 88.

FULL CIRCLE

Dresses and accessories have been and remain more than mere articles of clothing for Native women—they are canvases for the expression of tribal culture and personal identity. At each stage of life, exquisitely crafted clothing enriched the lives of its makers and those for whom they cared. Upon becoming an elder, a woman was recognized as a keeper of artistic, spiritual, historical, and everyday knowledge, which she passed on to younger generations. The cycle of learning had come full circle.

Contemporary Native women continue to be honored and celebrated in their communities for their achievements and contributions. Keri Jhane Myers illustrates this tradition with a memorable experience from her own life:

> The highest honor bestowed on a Comanche woman who had achieved many good things in her life was the distinctive gifting and wearing of an otterskin cap. A woman has to cross a lot of paths in her life in order to get this cap. When a woman wears an otter hat, the eagle plume she received in her adolescent years is typically worn on the back of the cap. We had a little ceremony in which my ninety-three-year-old aunt gave me an otter cap. You don't just make an otter cap and start wearing it. You have to achieve certain things in life. For me, it was a big honor. The elder people in my family felt that it was time I had an otter hat. I am a young person for this honor because I am forty-two. I didn't think I would get one until I was fifty or sixty.

Keri Jhane Myers
(Comanche), 2005.

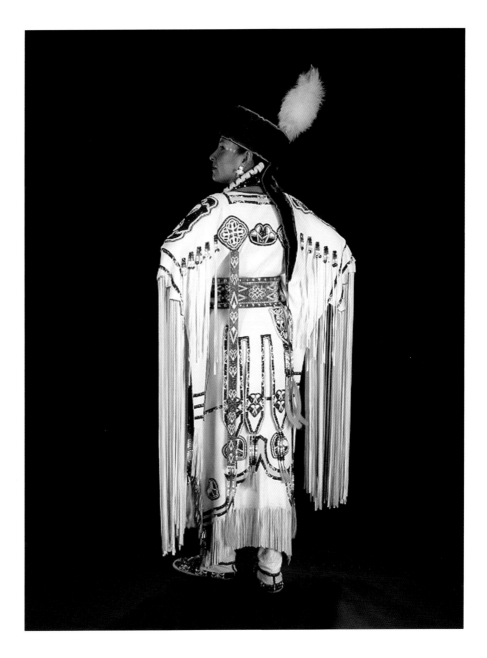

The highest honor
bestowed on a
Comanche woman
who had achieved
many good things
in her life was the
distinctive gifting
and wearing of an ot-
terskin cap. A woman
has to cross a lot of
paths in her life in
order to get this cap.

A Native woman's traditional dress today remains a symbol of her evolving
cultural identity, communicating solidarity with her adaptive, resilient people
and manifesting a shared sense of beauty and spirit. Yet tribal styles are supple
enough that this magnificent clothing still expresses the artist's personal beliefs, emotions, and experiences throughout her dance of life.

Comanche three-hide
dress and accessories,
ca. 1890. Oklahoma.
Hide, seed beads, tin
cones, sinew, thread,
harness leather, German
silver, silver metallic
spots, yellow and red
paint, rawhide. 2/1803,
23/208, RP1643, 2/1501

At first glance, the three
beaded bands on the
cape of this Comanche
dress are similar to
those of a Cheyenne-
style dress. Comanche
artists, however, use a
different beading tech-
nique, sometimes called
"flat gourd stitch,"
wherein they attach each
bead individually to the
dress. As a result, the
beadwork lies flat
against the surface.

NOTES

1. Unless otherwise noted, all quotations from contemporary artists in this essay derive from interviews conducted with the artists by Emil Her Many Horses and Colleen Cutschall at NMAI's National Powwow in Washington, D.C., August 2005, and at NMAI in December 2005.

2. Alice C. Fletcher and Francis La Flesche, *The Omaha Tribe*, Vol. 2 (Lincoln: University of Nebraska Press, 1992), 494, 503. This edition was reproduced from the *Twenty-Seventh Annual Report of the Bureau of American Ethnology to the Secretary of the Smithsonian Institution, 1905–1906* (Washington, D.C.: Government Printing Office, 1911).

3. Robin Ridington, "Omaha Images of Renewal," *Canadian Journal of Native Studies* 7, no. 2 (1987): 160–61.

4. Clark Wissler, *Decorative Art of the Sioux Indians* [Bulletin of the American Museum of Natural History 18, no. 3] (New York: American Museum of Natural History, 1904), 242.

5. Jay Miller, ed., *Mourning Dove: A Salishan Autobiography* (Lincoln: University of Nebraska Press, 1990), 64.

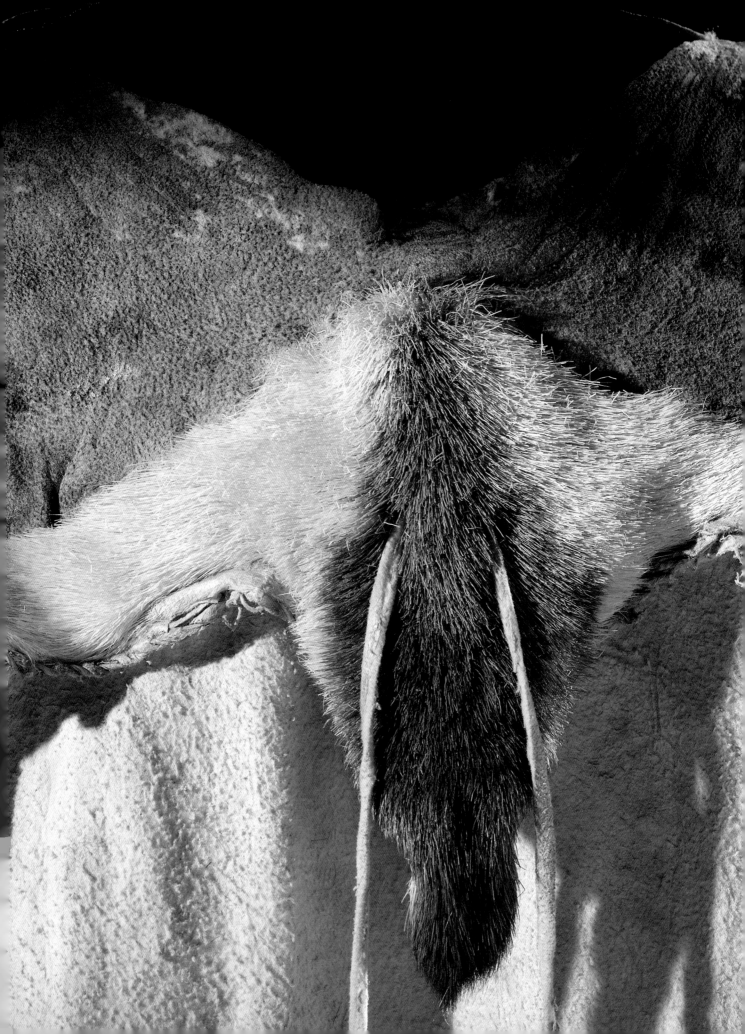

The Invisible Dress

It is tanned deerhide. Sometimes it is too large
because the Great Mothers made this two-tail dress
for a powerful purpose. Constructed with water,
with brains, with trees, with bone scrapers,
it was imbued with thoughts for protection and legacies.

They evoked the stars, the light with symbols,
patterned behavior with song. This is given in Dream.
The tones focused luminous depictions of story.
Neither flesh nor labor are empty of reflection.
Think of the Deer.

It is appropriate to cover with the handiwork of survival.
The Great Fathers brought this passage about, safely
in their hands. Infinite in this dress, together,
brought down by inexplicable violence and hardship,
we emerge, again, wearing this dress, necessary
and radiantly fearless.

Arikara two-hide dress
(detail). See p. 29.

Creativity and Cosmopolitanism:
Women's Enduring Traditions

JANET CATHERINE BERLO

IN PLAINS, PLATEAU, AND GREAT BASIN CULTURES, a dress is not simply a utilitarian garment. Its functionality extends into metaphysics; its artistry links human and spiritual realms. In the Lakota language, *saiciye* is the term for adorning oneself in traditional fashion, in a way that is pleasing to denizens of both the spirit world and the human world.[1]

Maintaining a connection to ancestral ways of knowing, and embodying that knowledge through proper relationships with relatives and with the natural world, continues to be important to Native people today.[2] Making and wearing ceremonial dress is a literal embodiment of ancestral knowledge. Women's dress encapsulates information about the world of animals (how to skin a deer and tan its hide; how to pluck, dye, and shape porcupine quills into ornament) and exemplifies the web of relationships among relatives, neighbors, and trading partners (honoring a child or a new daughter-in-law by making her a beautiful garment; demonstrating one's creativity and cosmopolitanism by incorporating materials from distant places into one's dress).

This essay considers some of the aesthetic and spiritual functions of Plains, Plateau, and Great Basin dresses, both in historic times and in the present. I shall also explore how Native dress—not only today but more than 200 years ago—presents a complex and constantly changing mix of traditional local knowledge combined with materials from long-distance trade. Indeed, the combination of these two—the local and the global—produced the works of great beauty and creativity in the National Museum of the American Indian (NMAI) collection, and in the personal collections of indigenous beadwork artists and dressmakers today.

Cheyenne cloth dress (detail). See p. 111.

ANCESTRAL WAYS OF KNOWING:
AESTHETIC AND METAPHYSICAL FOUNDATIONS FOR WOMEN'S ARTS

Following traditional aesthetics means you have to strive. You have to strive, not for perfection, but you have to strive for quality. You have to strive in a sense not for personal worthiness, but for an honoring statement to the Creator for what He has given you—to give respect to everything He has provided.

—Joanne Bigcrane (Pend d'Oreilles)[3]

Traditional hide dresses of the Plains and Plateau are characterized by beautiful beaded yokes—the area that covers the chest, shoulders, and upper back (see pp. 99, 100). On Lakota dresses, the sumptuous beading on the yokes is often blue, referring to water. The neck and head of the wearer emerge from the watery realm, and sometimes an abstract form of a turtle is beaded at the middle front of the yoke (see p. 101). Wearing such a dress alludes, in an abstract manner, to creation and procreation. Other Plains dresses allude to life and generativity by the way in which the techniques of constructing a two-hide dress focus the eye on the tail of a deer on the folded yoke (see p. 94). This highlights the fact that the dress was made from a living creature, some of whose life force continues to resonate even after it has been transformed for human use. (See Emil Her Many Horses' essay in this book for two-hide dress discussion.)

For many women, the skills used in making a dress are thought to be conferred

Nez Perce two-hide pattern dress with fully beaded yoke, ca. 1920. Idaho. Hide, canvas, cut glass beads, sinew, thread. 22/581

Cree and Ojibwe women married to French voyageurs were known as the Red River Métis people of Manitoba, Canada. Between 1820 and 1860, they developed a semi-floral embroidery style using quills, beads, and silk. Eventually, this floral beadwork style spread to the Northern Plains as Eastern tribes started to move westward. Bead designs were influenced by missionary vestments, church decoration, and European clothing and upholstery fabrics.

Sioux two-hide pattern
dress with fully beaded
yoke, ca. 1900. South
Dakota. Hide, seed
beads, sinew. 20/2210

Sioux artists are well-
known for their fully
beaded yokes. The yoke
is often light blue, repre-
senting a lake. The de-
signs are reflections of
clouds, and the narrow
white band is the shore.
In the center, a beaded
U-shaped design repre-
sents a turtle. Histori-
cally, the Sioux believed
that turtles had the
power to protect a
woman's health.

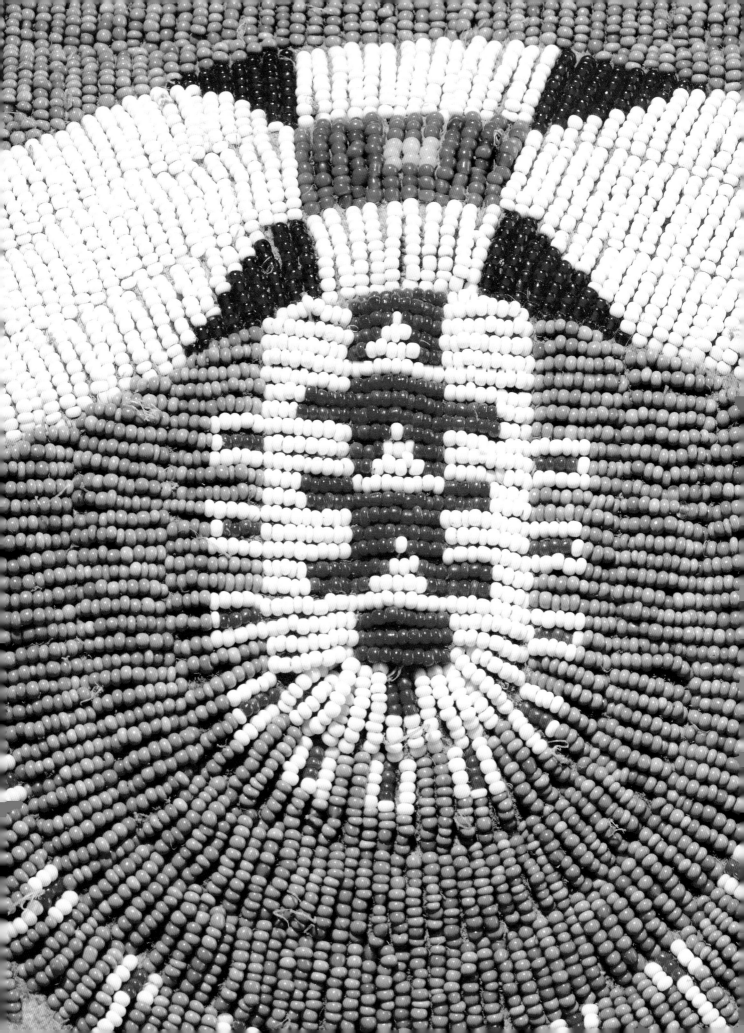

from the spirit world. In the stories of the Shuswap people of the northern Plateau of British Columbia, a holy person called simply "Old One" came into camp as a stranger and was well taken care of. In return, he gave to the people four bundles containing porcupine quills, woodpecker scalps, eagle tail feathers, and dentalium shells. He told them, "Hitherto, the value of these things has not been known, and people have not used them. Henceforth they will be much used and highly prized by all peoples for decorative purposes."[4]

Among the Lakota, one of the well-known stories is that of the supernatural figure of Double Woman who appeared to a young woman in a dream and taught her how to use quills for artistry. (For the Lakota, as for many Native peoples, dreaming is a noble way to receive sacred knowledge, so the art of quillwork is imbued with special legitimacy because of this origin.) After her dream, the young woman requested a tipi, a porcupine, and a prepared buffalo hide. She went out onto the land to find natural dyes of red, blue, yellow, and black. She entered her tipi and worked alone, emerging only for meals. She plucked the porcupine quills, separated them according to length, and dyed them. Eventually she invited one of her friends into the tipi and shared with her this new form of artistry. Together they quilled an entire buffalo robe, prepared a feast, and invited many other women. They sang sacred songs, and explained this marvelous new art to their peers.[5]

Cheyenne women traditionally did quillwork and beadwork within the structure of an artistic guild—a place for learning and for recognition of excellence. A woman would make a vow in front of the assembled members, stating her intention to embark on an ambitious project. The women gathered in one place to work on their sacred arts were thought to represent a substantial amount of spiritual power—so much so that a young Cheyenne warrior might dare to make a "raid" into their tipi: "A very brave man who had counted many coups might go up to the lodge door, strike the lodge, and counting a coup might enter and take a pot of the food standing by the fire, and carry it away with him." [6]

All of this illustrates that any sort of differentiation into realms of "secular" and "sacred" when it comes to women's dress is completely misguided. While at first consideration items of clothing might be characterized as secular, in fact, the making and wearing of aesthetically pleasing garments has for centuries held a deeply spiritual place in Native women's lives. In Lakota ritual, one might sing "Something sacred wears me"—a reversal of the expected.[7] The individual wears sacred garments and thus the sacred forces "wear" or animate the individual.

Yakama two-hide dress, ca. 1860. Probably Washington. Deerhide, elk teeth, faceted "Russian" glass beads, seed beads, pony beads, red wool, sinew. 19/6773

The beaded fringe on the yoke is typical of Plateau-style dresses. The large beads strung on the fringe are called "Russian" or "Siberian" beads. Russians traded them in North America, but they originated in Italy and Bohemia (now the Czech Republic).

So what constitutes an aesthetics of sacred or ceremonial dress? To my knowledge, no substantial inquiry into indigenous aesthetics has been conducted on the Plateau, Plains, or Great Basin. Yet Barbara Tedlock's work with contemporary Zuni people might suggest some shared preferences with other indigenous people of the west. Tedlock points out that in Zuni aesthetics, dynamic asymmetry is valued over exact balance; that mixtures of all sorts are always preferred to compositions of similar items (for example, a mixed bouquet rather than a dozen red roses); and that multiple textures and colors are the prevailing aesthetic across many domains, from cuisine to dress, dance, and performance.[8]

Many dresses demonstrate a preference for complex mixtures of materials, both local and exotic. This combination of objects from diverse sources was surely part of the aesthetic system of the Plains, Plateau, and Great Basin. A dress hanging in solitary splendor on a dress form in a museum display conveys a mistaken impression. In real life, on the special occasions on which many of these dresses were worn, the dress was part of an ensemble that may have included headgear, earrings, necklaces, shawls, bags, belts, leggings, and moccasins. Sally Shuster, a Yakama woman, posed for a photograph around 1900 that reveals the rich, multilayered aesthetic dimensions of formal dress (see p. 104, left). Over a printed calico dress (visible on the sleeve on the left arm), she wears a Plateau-style dress with large, bold bands of light and dark beadwork curving across the yoke. Over this, Shuster wears a Great Lakes-style beaded bandolier bag. In each hand, she carries a Plateau-style flat bag. Beaded fringes dangle from the bandolier bag as well as from her dress. Her long braids of hair (which seem to be wrapped in fur) hang down over her dress. Huge pen-

dant shell earrings, a choker, and several necklaces of beads add to the mélange of layers, textures, colors, and multicultural effect. The aesthetic pleasure seems to consist of the very personalized bringing together of all of these items.

Like Sally Shuster, the young Wishram woman in Edward Curtis's famous 1910 photo displays her wealth and elegance in a multisensory display (see above, right). Over a sprigged calico dress (visible on her right arm), she wears a dress of tanned hide with rows of dark and light beadwork on the bodice. Each "lazy-stitch" (wherein the beadworker picks up multiple beads on her needle before attaching the thread back down on the hide) consists of a dozen beads, causing the beadwork to move and gap, rather than to lie flat against the bodice. Over the hide dress, she wears a number of beaded necklaces—dark and light, long and short. At the bottom of her beaded yoke, pendant fringes of different types of beads and olivella shells hang down over her belt. Her long earrings and the headdress that cascades over her forehead are both fashioned from beads, dentalium shells, and Chinese coins (see p. 114 for a discussion of such coins). When she walked, all would be in motion, the coins on her forehead glinting in the sun.

Left: Yakama woman Sally Shuster photographed by Lee Moorhouse, ca. 1900.

Right: Wishram woman photographed by Edward S. Curtis in 1910.

Tawny Hale (Navajo/Lakota), left, and Danita Goodwill (Osage) in cloth dresses at the NMAI National Pow-wow at the MCI (Verizon) Center in Washington, D.C., August 2005.

Opposite: Kiowa Battle Dress (detail). See p. 138.

Blackfeet dress (detail). See p. 84.

In many of the dresses in this book, shine and flash are prized: silk ribbon provides a gleaming surface against the matte of a woolen dress; thimbles, coins, and brass beads would have started their lives as shiny golden and silver items, before they became tarnished. These metallic additions and the brass and tin cone-shaped tinklers on many dresses would have added an aural dimension to the ensemble as well.

The ostentatious display of a layered accumulation of garments and objects is indigenous to the Plains, Plateau, and Great Basin, and to both men and women. When George Catlin sought to paint a portrait of Máh-to-tóh-pa in the 1830s, the artist noted that he had to ask the Mandan chief to remove some of his panoply of garments and accoutrements so that the portrait would be visually comprehensible; Catlin strove for "grace and simplicity" in the portrait, which was decidedly not the self-presentation that Máh-to-tóh-pa sought (see p. 108). Catlin wrote that Máh-to-tóh-pa "was beautifully and extravagantly dressed, and in this he was not alone, for hundreds of others are equally elegant."[9]

The trenchancy of Catlin's statement, as well as my characterization of a multidimensional aesthetic of dress, can be observed any summer at Crow Fair in Montana (see pp. 38, 39), or at any powwow across North America (see p. 105). It is also evident in many of the dresses in this book.

Art historian Kate Duncan has characterized contemporary Plateau beadwork in terms of its "bold—even flamboyant—forms, bright colors, and force-

George Catlin (1796–1872),
*Máh-to-tóh-pa, Four Bears,
Second Chief, in Full Dress*,
1832. Oil on canvas,
73.7 x 60.9 cm.
Smithsonian American Art
Museum, Gift of Mrs.
Joseph Harrison, Jr.
1985.66.128

ful contrasts." She has described the beadwork on many historical dresses as "elegant syncopations that counter differing width bands of colored beads with bands of the white horn-shaped dentalium shells, tightly interlocking bands of texture within a grid of opposing bands of color."[10] While each region and each tribe of the Plains, Plateau, and Great Basin has long had its own characteristic style, the extensive history of intertribal trade and intertribal celebratory gatherings, such as the powwow, have ensured that great diversity is the aesthetic norm almost everywhere.

CENTURIES OF COSMOPOLITANISM AND CREATIVITY IN WOMEN'S CLOTHING

When I attend Schemitzun Powwow in Connecticut, I spend a day on my way home in New York. I go to the Fashion District and look at all the trim. I look at all the different types of cloth, for a really unique dress to make. We get our rhinestones there. And we don't buy just a yard of rhinestones. We buy them ten yards at a time. You look at the things available, and how you could incorporate them while keeping to a type of tradition.

—Keri Jhane Myers (Comanche)[11]

Contemporary dressmaker and dancer Keri Jhane Myers' words, though at first glance seemingly "nontraditional," accurately reflect hundreds of years of artistic practice on the Plains, Plateau, and Great Basin. When imagining these regions circa 1800, our thinking is all too often limited by words such as "traditional" or "authentic." Too many people imagine "pristine" American Indian societies somehow hermetically sealed away from outside influences when, in fact, the vectors of global mercantilism extended into western North America from all directions—north, south, east, and west.

In contrast, when imagining European or Chinese societies in 1800, we are well aware of their cosmopolitan nature, and the complex intercultural trade that brought them diverse goods. Since ancient times, the Silk Road has linked disparate societies from the ancient Mediterranean to Afghanistan to China. Valued materials, including fabrics, spices, semiprecious stones, and animals changed hands along the Silk Road.[12] It should not be surprising that in the New World, too, ancient trade routes set the path for the routes followed by non-Native explorers and traders. In prehistoric times, valued stones and shells were traded over long distances (see p. 110). Innovative artistic ideas, too, were disseminated by means of goods that changed hands over hundreds of miles. Pecos Pueblo (in present-day New Mexico) was the crossroads of exchange for goods traveling between Mexico, the Southwest, and the Plains. French-Canadian traders and fur trappers traversed Lake Superior and the Canadian prairies to reach the Upper Missouri region and the Northwest. Goods from the West Coast, and even from China, reached the interior through the trading center long-established at The Dalles, on the Columbia River (in present-day Oregon), which one early nineteenth-century fur trader characterized as "the great emporium or mart of the Columbia."[13] This panoply of materials from the global marketplace is reflected in Native women's dress.[14]

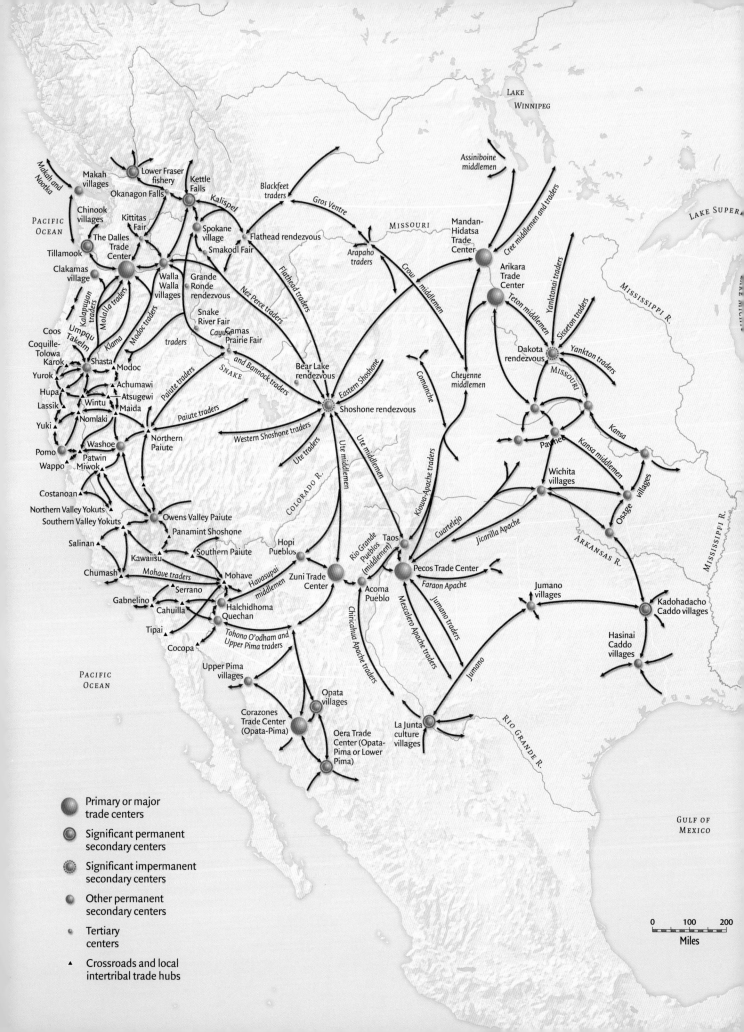

LAKE
WINNIPEG

LAKE SUPER

PACIFIC
OCEAN

Makah and
Nootka

Makah
villages

Lower Fraser
fishery

Okanagon Falls

Kettle
Falls

Kalispel

Blackfeet
traders

Gros Ventre

MISSOURI

Mandan-
Hidatsa
Trade
Center

Cree middlemen and traders

Chinook villages

Kittitas
Fair

Spokane
village

Flathead rendezvous

Arapaho
traders

Arikara
Trade
Center

Yanktonai traders

The Dalles
Trade
Center

Walla
Walla
villages

Smakodl Fair

Teton middlemen

Tillamook

Grande
Ronde
rendezvous

Flathead traders

Nez Perce traders

Crow middlemen

Sisseton traders

Clakamas
village

Kalapuyan
traders

Molalla traders

Snake
River Fair

Camas
Prairie Fair

MISSISSIPPI R.

Coos

Umpqu
Takelm

Klama

Modoc traders

Cayuse

Dakota
rendezvous

Yankton traders

Coquille-
Tolowa
Karok

Shasta

Modoc

traders

and Bannock traders

Bear Lake
rendezvous

MISSOURI

Yurok

Achumawi

Eastern Shoshone

Cheyenne
middlemen

Yankton traders

Hupa

Atsugewi

SNAKE

Shoshone rendezvous

Lassik

Wintu

Maida

Comanche

Nomlaki

Paiute traders

Kansa

Yuki

Western Shoshone traders

Pawnee

Kansa middlemen

Pomo

Washoe

Northern
Paiute

Ute traders

Wichita
villages

Osage
villages

Wappo

Patwin
Miwok

Ute middlemen

Kiowa-Apache traders

Costanoan

COLORADO R.

Northern Valley Yokuts

Southern Valley Yokuts

Owens Valley Paiute

Rio Grande
Pueblos
(middlemen)

Taos

Cuartelejo

ARKANSAS R.

Panamint Shoshone

Hopi
Pueblos

Jicarilla Apache

Salinan

Southern Paiute

Zuni Trade
Center

Pecos Trade Center

MISSISSIPPI R.

Kawaiisu

Mohave traders

Mohave

Havasupai
middlemen

Acoma
Pueblo

Faraon Apache

Chumash

Serrano

Halchidhoma

Zuni Trade
Center

Jumano
villages

Jumano traders

Kadohadacho
Caddo villages

Gabnelino

Cahuilla

Quechan

Chiricahua Apache traders

Mescalero Apache traders

Jumano

Hasinai
Caddo
villages

Tipai

Cocopa

Tohono O'odham and
Upper Pima traders

Jumano

Upper Pima
villages

Opata
villages

RIO GRANDE R.

PACIFIC
OCEAN

Corazones
Trade Center
(Opata-Pima)

Oera Trade
Center (Opata-
Pima or Lower
Pima)

La Junta
culture villages

GULF OF
MEXICO

Primary or major
trade centers

Significant permanent
secondary centers

Significant impermanent
secondary centers

Other permanent
secondary centers

Tertiary
centers

Crossroads and local
intertribal trade hubs

0   100   200

Miles

Every trader's journal or inventory book in the eighteenth and nineteenth century lists substantial stocks of beads for use in trade. Vivid large blue beads and dazzling white beads were the first; indeed, William Clark (of the Lewis and Clark Expedition) remarked that "blue beads occupy the place which gold has with us. White beads may be considered as our silver."[15] Later, beads in numerous hues transformed women's ornamentation of hides, as many of the illustrations in this book demonstrate. Though beadwork seems laborious to us today, these durable and nonfading materials were a labor-saving revelation to women who previously had to hunt porcupines, pluck the quills, and then dye and soften the quills. Only then could they do the embroidered, wrapped, and stitched work required to ornament a robe or dress.

This map (from *Handbook of North American Indians*, Vol. 4, 1988, with updated graphics) shows both permanent trade centers and seasonal ones (such as the Shoshone and Dakota rendezvous) by which Native and non-Native traders moved goods across long distances. Such economic interconnections were established long before the coming of Europeans to western North America; in many instances, European trade routes were simply superimposed on top of ancient indigenous ones. By means of such long-distance trade, products from Europe and China permeated deep into the West even before extensive settlement by outsiders.

Cheyenne cloth dress, ca. 1910. Probably Montana. Rainbow selvage red wool, dentalium shells, ribbon, thread. 6/4020

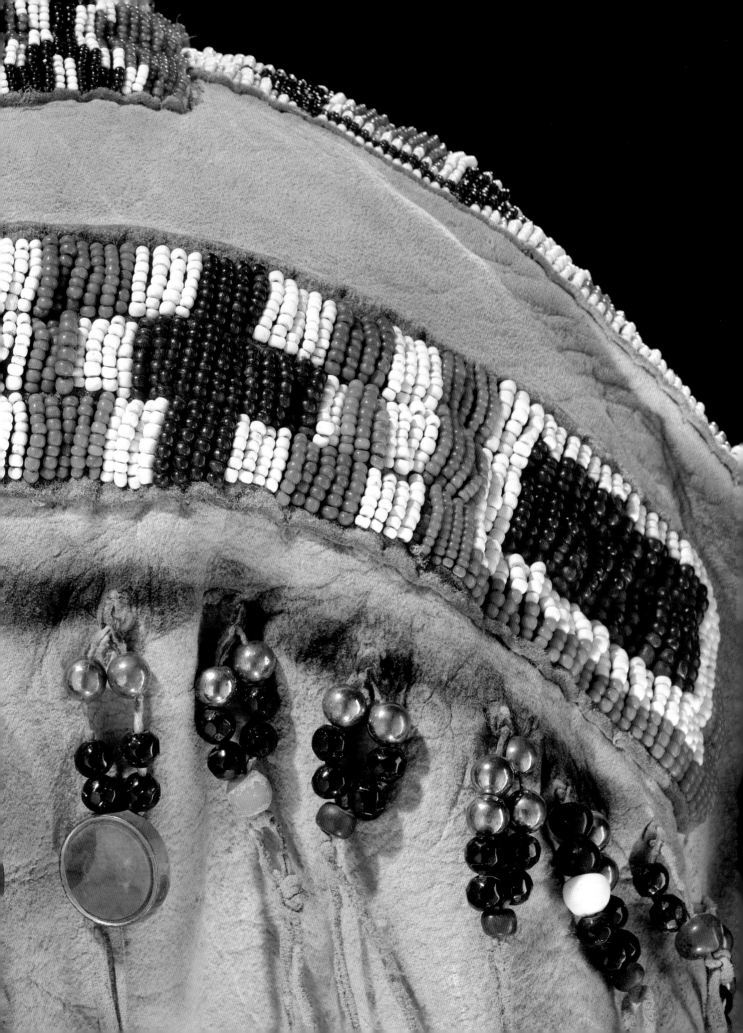

Blackfoot two-hide dress (detail). See p. 34.

Opposite and pp. 112–113 (detail of back of dress): Comanche girl's three-hide dress, ca. 1860. Oklahoma. Hide, pony beads, various trade beads, seed beads, yellow and green paint, coins, shells, tin cones, sinew. 2/2585

Along with beads from Venice and Czechoslovakia, traders filled their packs with shiny brass buttons, buckles, and thimbles. Needles and awls to aid in beadwork and other clothing arts were also included. Lengths of sturdy red and blue wool cloth, as well as printed calicos, silk ribbons, and cotton bandanas, were offered, as were a multitude of shell ornaments, some Native-made and some manufactured by non-Natives for the Indian trade.[16] Dentalium shells—hollow, curving, horn-like shells from one to four inches long—were delicate-looking but durable, and sought after for clothing and jewelry. Harvested off the west coast of Vancouver Island by the Nootka people, they were traded in standard strings of forty shells to both Native and non-Native traders who sold them at The Dalles.[17] More than 3,000 of these shells ornament the dress on p. 111.

On the Northwest Coast, Chinese coins with holes in them (nicknamed "China cash") were a part of the circulating system of trade that extended from Boston to the fur-trade ports of the Pacific Northwest to Canton from the 1780s to the 1840s. Some of these made their way inland through The Dalles as well.[18]

Native dressmakers examined buttons, thimbles, and Chinese coins, and looked beyond their utilitarian function. They saw durable and shiny ornaments to add to their repertory of quill and bead artistry. These metallic goods added flair and flash to hide garments (see pp. 112–113). And precious bits of red wool cloth were sometimes chosen to add staccato color highlights (see above). Red materials and pigments were especially valued in these regions, so much so that an essential part of any trader's inventory was at least a few dozen packets of Chinese vermilion (see p. 118).

Sioux cloth dress, ca. 1900. South Dakota. Saved-list blue wool, dentalium shells, German silver brooch pins, ribbon, brass sequins, thread. 2/6425; Sicangu Lakota (Sioux) earrings, ca. 1890. South Dakota. Dentalium shells, brass hoops and spots, German silver pendants, rawhide, sinew. 13/6496; Sicangu Lakota (Sioux) choker, ca. 1890. South Dakota. Dentalium shells, brass spots, rawhide, sinew. 13/6497; Oglala Lakota (Sioux) leggings, ca. 1880. South Dakota. Hide, seed beads, sinew. 18/4293; Sioux moccasins, ca. 1890. South Dakota. Hide, seed beads, rawhide, sinew. 25/107; Sioux knife sheath and belt, ca. 1880. South Dakota. Harness leather, brass tacks, commercial buckle. 21/1916

As cloth became more plentiful—and hides more scarce—women made loose, semi-tailored dresses. The ones of wool provided warmth, and the yokes of the finest could easily be ornamented with local items, such as elk teeth (see p. 122), or dentalium shells from the Pacific. Silk ribbons and buckles sometimes punctuated the appliqué of hundreds of teeth or shells (see p. 116 and above). Canadian trader François-Antoine Larocque, trading with the Flatheads (Salish) in 1805, noted that elk teeth were so highly prized that seventy to eighty of them were worth one horse. He also observed that "whenever they get a brass kettle from their neighbours, they do not use it for culinary purposes, but cut it into small pieces with which they ornament and decorate their garments and their hair."[19] His remark held true across the entire West.

VERMILION: "CHINESE RED" IN THE FUR TRADE

Vermilion pigment provides yet another example of the scope of global mercantilism evident in the American West in the eighteenth and nineteenth centuries. The southwestern Chinese province of Kweichow (Guizhou) has long been known for producing the valuable and brilliant red pigment derived from mercury and known as vermilion. This was one of the fundamental stocks of the Indian trader across North America. In the nineteenth century, it was usually sold in small amounts, packaged in paper stamped with Chinese characters, like those pictured here, which were collected in Montana among the Piegan Blackfeet.

Vermilion was costly for the trader. He, in turn, marked it up so that it was even costlier for his Native customers.[20] The literal translation of the Lakota term for adorning oneself in a ritually correct manner, *saiciye*, is "to paint oneself red." Red pigment was widely used across North America as a sacred color for painting both the human body and hide clothing.

Packets of Chinese vermilion pigment collected among the Piegan, ca. 1880. Montana. 22/1841

Blackfoot cloth dress, ca. 1910. Canada. Red cloth, basket beads, brass thimbles and bells, muslin, thread. 14/9292

Made entirely of European trade materials and influenced by Western fashion (with longer sleeves and a defined waist), this artist's dress still follows the traditional "tail" outline of a hide with the downward dip of basket beads.

NATIVE WOMEN'S DRESSES   **119**

Women were by no means simply the recipients of the largesse of the traders—they had a key economic role to play in the transactions of the fur trade, for they were the ones who processed the hides and furs that were the source of the traders' wealth. The sheer number of hides shipped to just one city can only suggest the magnitude of their industry: "By the 1840s, over 90,000 buffalo robes poured into St. Louis annually, and this increased to an average of 100,000 robes per year for the 1850s."[21] Traders often married Native women, forging an economic partnership that profited both husband and wife. At some trading centers, such as The Dalles, women seem to have conducted the trade in the goods that other women would buy.[22]

Goods from the international market did not, by any means, completely replace intertribal trade. Indigenous raw materials (such as dentalium shells) and finished goods (such as moccasins and woven blankets) continued to travel these routes as well. Sioux moccasins were highly prized across the Plains, Plateau, and Great Basin. And boldly patterned Navajo blankets from the distant Southwest were sought and worn by men and women alike. Evidence of their value on the Great Plains is found in an early watercolor by Karl Bodmer; in Kiowa, Cheyenne, and Lakota ledger drawings; and in late nineteenth-century photographs. While traveling on the Upper Missouri River with Prince Maximilian's expedition in 1832–34, Bodmer endeavored to portray the Native peoples he encountered as "untainted" by outside influence, yet he unwittingly painted a Piegan Blackfeet man wearing a striped Navajo blanket and a Pueblo silver pendant—both objects of long-distance trade.[23] In one of the Lakota Winter Counts (a pictographic historical record), the winter of 1858–59 was characterized as a "Many-Navajo-blankets winter." Several sources agree that a notable influx of these prized textiles occurred at that time.[24]

A Navajo First Phase Chief Blanket in NMAI's collection was acquired by artist DaCost Smith while he traveled and painted among the Sioux in 1884.[25] The Sioux owner of this blanket transformed it according to local custom by attaching brass and German silver buttons, quill-wrapped cords, horsehair, and tin ornaments (see p. 121). Moreover, there is some visual evidence that a local beaded blanket strip of the kind normally seen on Northern Plains hides and blankets had been attached to it at one time. When worn with a trade cloth dress, it attested to the cosmopolitanism of its wearer. A portrait of Sioux woman Alice Lone Bear shows her wearing another such Navajo blanket, along with a cloth dress decorated with elk teeth, a pipe bead necklace, and a drop decorated with metal disks (see p. 124, top).

Navajo trade blanket, ca. 1850. Arizona. Dyed yarn, brass and German silver conchos, quill-wrapped fringe, horsehair, tin cones. 20/1339

All of these examples reveal that cosmopolitanism clearly was a traditional aspect of artistry in the indigenous West. The fur trade was a mechanism that allowed this cosmopolitan aesthetic to reach new heights by the early nineteenth century. The diverse and stylish garments created for dance and ceremony by Native women today further emphasize that Native artistry takes excellent advantage of all available materials.

HONORING ACHIEVEMENT: GENDER, VALOR, POWER

When I wear my dresses, I feel a really strong sense of accomplishment because a lot of work has gone into them. I want to make dresses that last as long as the antiques I see now.

—Jamie Okuma (Luiseño/Shoshone-Bannock)

In Native societies, women bring honor on themselves and their families by their industry, creativity, and generosity, and are rewarded for their hard work. This is as true today as it was two hundred years ago. (See, for example, Keri Jhane Myers' remarks on receiving an otterskin cap, in Cutschall essay, p. 90.) In the historic era, men and women had parallel paths by which to gain honor and prestige. Men honored their families by being good hunters, by participating in ceremony, and by conducting themselves bravely in war-making and horse-capture raids. They recorded such events on buffalo robes, skin shirts, and in small autobiographical drawings.[26] Such items provided pictorial evidence that backed up oral recitations of brave deeds. Women honored their families by their comportment and industry. The ceremonial garments they made for themselves and their loved ones were the most creative examples of that industriousness. Among some tribes, such work was done within artistic guilds, elsewhere it was individual work, but always approached with seriousness and a prayerful attitude.

George Bird Grinnell, who lived among the Cheyenne in the 1890s, observed of quill- and beadwork, "this work women considered of high importance, and when properly performed, quite as creditable as were bravery and success in war among men." He noted that in the meetings of the Cheyenne Quillwork Society, the assembled women recalled and described their previous fine works, "telling of the robes they had ornamented. This recital was formal in character, and among women closely paralleled the counting of coup by men."[27]

The amount of labor lavished on an outfit demonstrates the deep respect and love felt for an individual. To spend hundreds of hours making a beaded dress, or one ornamented with hundreds of elk teeth, for a male relative's new bride not only celebrated her arrival into the family but also honored her husband. In her old age, Buffalo Bird Woman (Hidatsa, ca. 1839–1932) recalled, "My husband's parents gave me an elk teeth dress with 375 elk teeth on it. Afterwards they gave me another with 600 elk teeth. Six times in my life have I owned elk teeth dresses."[28] Contemporary Crow artist Gladys Jefferson, while looking at

Crow elk tooth dress, ca. 1890. Montana. Red and green wool, imitation elk teeth (bone), seed beads, muslin, thread. 12/6406; Crow leggings, ca. 1890. Montana. Hide, blue and red wool, seed beads, sinew. 14/9546; Crow moccasins, ca. 1890. Montana. Hide, seed beads, rawhide, sinew. 11/8006; Crow belt, ca. 1900. Montana. Harness leather, seed beads, brass tacks, hide. 21/6853

Color lithograph of Alice Lone Bear (Sioux), 1898. Omaha, Nebraska. Photo by Frank A. Rinehart or Adolph F. Muhr. P11233

Arapaho woman at the U.S. Indian Congress, Trans-Mississippi and International Exposition, 1898. Omaha, Nebraska. Photo by Frank A. Rinehart or Adolph F. Muhr. N19287A

Gladys Jefferson (Crow) in her elk tooth dress, 2005.

As a young woman, Gladys was one of the first to participate in the Fancy Shawl Dance, introduced to pow-wows in the early 1960s. Over a period of more than 20 years, she won many contests and helped establish this style of dance.

some of the dresses in the NMAI collection, related, "A long time ago, the elk tooth dress wasn't worn every day. Back then, it was to outfit your daughter-in-law or your sister-in-law. It was basically a wedding dress. As a boy grew up, he would collect elk teeth and save them for his mother and sisters to put on a dress for his wife when he married."[29] Her own red cloth elk tooth dress is a valued item, and she wears it with turquoise jewelry from the Southwest of the sort that many cosmopolitan Natives wear today (see p. 125).

The historical dresses ornamented with many examples of the two prized eyeteeth of the elk were not only made for new daughters-in-law; some such dresses were made for precious girl children, too, as seen in a photograph of two small Cheyenne girls (top, left). Elk tooth ornamentation is not necessarily limited to the yoke and sleeves. On some dresses, the teeth continue down the body of the dress as well (see pp. 122, 128).

Fully beaded moccasins are another sign of honor and respect. Found in many museum collections, these are often said to be moccasins for the dead, yet many were made to honor a special living relative (see p. 127). In the biography of a twentieth-century Cheyenne woman, Mary Little Bear Inkanish, the authors relate that, "At the Sun Dance when Mary was about a year old, her aunt had a give-away in her honor. She had made Mary a pair of full-beaded moccasins—even the soles were beaded—to show that this little girl's family would not let her feet touch the ground if they could help it."[30]

Two Cheyenne girls wearing dresses made of wool cloth and decorated with elk teeth, 1915. Oklahoma. Photographer unknown. P14926

Cheyenne girl wearing an elaborate beaded dress and breastplate, 1915. Oklahoma. Photographer unknown. P14929

Sicangu Lakota (Sioux) girl's dress, ca. 1890. South Dakota. Hide, seed beads, tin cones, sinew. 16/2323; Sioux girl's moccasins, ca. 1900. South Dakota. Hide, seed beads, silver metallic beads, green cloth, sinew. 6/2015; Sioux girl's leggings, ca. 1895. South Dakota. Hide, seed beads, green paint, sinew. 9063; Sicangu Lakota (Sioux) girl's belt with accessories, ca. 1900. South Dakota. Hide, seed beads, horn, tin cones, horsehair, rawhide, sinew. 16/2518

This lavishly decorated dress, particularly the fully beaded skirt, shows the care taken by female relatives to clothe a child. It would have been worn on a very special occasion.

Crow elk tooth dress, ca. 1910. Montana. Blue and red wool, imitation elk teeth (bone), seed beads, muslin, thread. 12/6407

The triangular red wool panel around the neck opening of this Crow artist's dress was probably made to resemble the tail on hide dresses. Imitation elk teeth carved from bone are used since opportunities for elk hunting had declined by the end of the 19th century, by which time most Native peoples were confined to reservations or reserves in the U.S. and Canada.

Dora Old Elk (Assiniboine/Crow) at the NMAI National Powwow at the MCI (Verizon) Center in Washington, D.C., August 2005. Dora is the daughter of Georgianna Old Elk, pictured on p. 52.

Today, an ambitious dressmaker might honor her ancestors by making a garment that recalls their deeds; the wearing of it would serve as an occasion to remember and recount their generosity of spirit. Joyce Growing Thunder Fogarty (Assiniboine/Sioux) vowed to make a Sioux-style dress with full accessories, in honor of her grandparents Ben and Josephine Gray Hawk (see p. 131). The beaded imagery of horses with war bonnets is biographical:

Joyce Growing Thunder Fogarty (Assiniboine/Sioux), 2005.

> Back when I was growing up in the early '60s, my grandpa was one of the head leaders on our reservation.... He used to have giveaways because he had horses, a lot of horses. When he had an honoring for one of his grandkids, he always took a horse and tied a war bonnet on it. After they sang the honoring song, my grandfather would turn the horse loose. There would be men standing all around in the background with their ropes, and they would have to go on foot to catch the horse. He would let it go, and whoever caught it could have the horse and the war bonnet. And that's how he honored his grandchildren. So that's what I plan on doing with this dress—honoring my grandfather and grandmother.

The late reservation era (1890s–1920s) was a time of tremendous social pressure as Indians were pressed to renounce their indigenous ways in favor of assimilation. Native women launched their own subversively defiant response to this by creating some of the most complex beaded outfits ever seen in indigenous America. Lakota women, in particular, became well-known for their ostentatiously beaded garments. Some, especially made for children, were beaded all over and were weighty both in ornamentation and in meaning (see p. 127). They have been characterized as a response to extreme social disruption and the threat of assimilation.[31]

Lakota tradition credits the supernatural figure of Double Woman for the gift of quillwork. Just as a dream engendered this sacred art form, it is also said that if a woman dreams of Double Woman, she will excel at art, producing much quillwork of unsurpassed quality. Moreover, the dreamer herself might enjoy extraordinary powers:

Beaded detail and drawing for *Give Away Horses*, a dress created by Joyce Growing Thunder Fogarty in 2006 to honor her grandparents Ben and Josephine Gray Hawk.

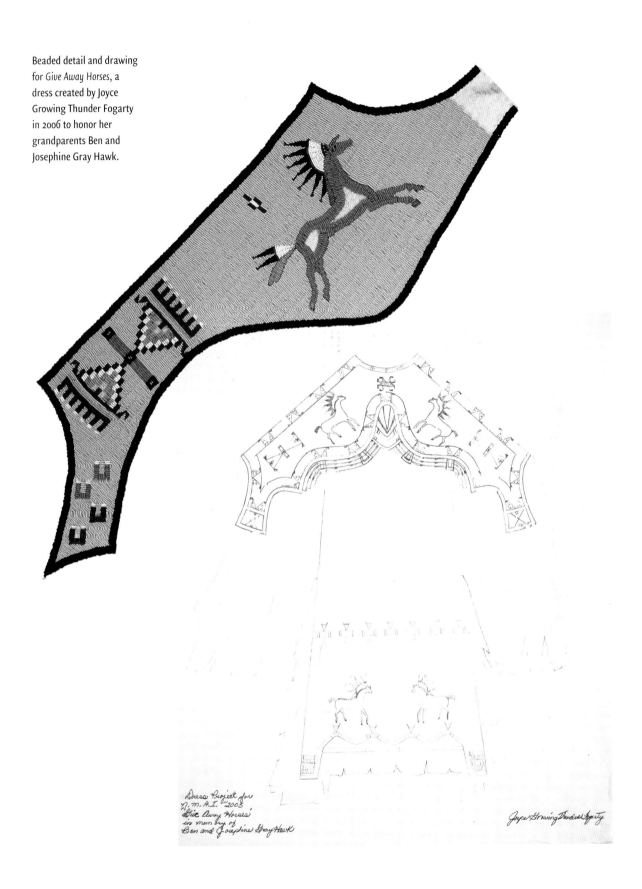

Dress Project for
N.M.A.I. "2005"
"Give Away Horses"
in memory of
Ben and Josephine Gray Hawk

Joyce Growing Thunder Fogarty

Sioux cloth dress, ca. 1900.
North Dakota. Muslin, red
wool, red, yellow, and
black paint, thread.
10/8371

She could do the quill or beadwork on one side of a pair of moccasins, place it against the blank one, sit on it, sing the song, and both would be done. Or she could even just put the quills between the moccasin blanks, sit on them, sing the song, and it would be finished.[32]

While perhaps one could not expect such supernatural intervention, a Crow story suggests that cooperation might save the day when a seemingly insurmountable task needs to be accomplished. In one tale, an unreasonable man warns his betrothed that he would marry her only if she were powerful enough to tan a buffalo hide and embellish it with quillwork in a single day. Female helpers of different species arrive to help her. Badgers and beavers stake the hide. Rats, moles, mice, ants, bees, and flies remove the flesh, scrape and soften it. A porcupine provides quills and, with the assistance of a bevy of ants, completes the embroidery and rolls it up for the woman to take home.[33] This cross-species cooperation can be viewed as a model for women's collaboration.

Kheri Jane Myers speaks enthusiastically about the value of group effort:

> In the wintertime, my friends and I sometimes get together and have a beading circle. We all sit together and work on things. I help them with their outfits, and they help me with my outfits. A lot of times we trade work.... It's good to have that collaboration, because sometimes when you're wearing a dress, you not only represent yourself but also your whole family.
>
> Nowadays, we don't live in a band, but we consider our close friends adoptive family. I have a friend that I call my sister. Many people don't understand, "Oh, sisters? You two don't look alike." But we're sisters because we've experienced things together in our lives. We've helped each other in different ways, in beadwork and beyond. So you are able to wear a dress that your sister put her love and her work into because she cares about you. If she didn't care about you, she wouldn't sit for hours and help you do this just so you can dance. To me, that's important.

On the Great Plains, in the eighteenth and nineteenth centuries, men's and women's clothing required cross-gender collaboration. Men would hunt the animals; women would dress the skins and construct the garments. While a man would paint his war record on his shirt, he would rely on a woman's artistry for the beadwork or quillwork on it. Sometimes people might transgress the gender boundaries. For example, there are many male beadworkers today, and perhaps there were some in the nineteenth century. While usually only men painted narrative scenes, a woman might do so occasionally. Among the Blackfoot, in the early twentieth century, anthropologist Walter McClintock documented an instance in which the wife of Big Eyes "painted pictures of both war and hunting ... illustrating adventures in the life of her husband."[34] Most probably he gave her the right to do this because she was a better artist than he.

Three unusual dresses painted with narrative scenes (see pp. 132, 135, 136) suggest either cross-gender collaboration, or else transgression of gender roles. Each dress is made of muslin, with cloth or ribbon in other colors added as trim. Each depicts scenes of men engaged in warfare or horse-capture. At the end of the nineteenth century and the beginning of the twentieth, many such scenes were painted on lengths of muslin used as tipi liners or made for sale.[35] But the painting of war records on women's dresses is rare. Such dresses were said to be "permitted only to those whose relatives have been killed in battle"[36];

Hunkpapa Lakota (Sioux) cloth dress, ca. 1890. North Dakota. Muslin, ribbons, red and blue wool, red, black, blue, and yellow paint, thread. 21/3665; Sioux belt, ca. 1900. South Dakota or North Dakota. German silver conchos, commercial buckle, harness leather. 1/3390

Sioux cloth dress, ca. 1890. South Dakota. Muslin, blue denim, red wool, red, green, and black paint, thread. 17/6078

in the only well-documented case, a Mandan dress was made by a woman and painted by her husband with scenes of his own war exploits and that of the woman's brother.[37] We can only assume that the dresses illustrated here are similar. On the dress on p. 136, large paintings of bullet holes with blood-red pigment flowing from them are painted in a scale appropriate to the dress itself, while small-scale scenes of warfare take place around them. Presumably, the painted bullet holes mark the anatomical areas where the wearer's male relative was shot.

Could women have painted these? Possibly; yet it is more likely that a man painted the dress that the wife or sister of a valiant warrior wore, in order that she could proclaim the brave deeds of her relatives by dancing in such a dress. Women of many Plains cultures in the nineteenth century conducted warrior dances in which they donned male regalia. This tradition of publicly honoring the valor of a husband or brother has by no means died out.

Kiowa people, for example, know from family history that in the nineteenth century, a woman would honor her warrior husband by dancing with his accoutrements of war or his war trophies; this appears as a subject in Kiowa ledger art, too. One drawing done in the 1880s depicts five Kiowa women dancing to the singing and drumming of five men who face them (see p. 139). Each woman holds or wears an item of war regalia—a headdress, lance, or bow. Their faces are painted, and they wear red and blue trade cloth dresses, some with aprons or blankets.

Kiowa women today carry on the tradition of honoring men who have served in the U.S. military; a small number of them have the right to do so by wearing a copyrighted item of clothing—the Battle Dress (see p. 138). Vanessa Jennings can recite a litany of ancestors and relatives who have died or been injured in every war since the late nineteenth century, including World Wars I and II and Vietnam. She says:

Kiowa Battle Dress, ca. 2000, and belt with drop, 2006. Made by Vanessa Jennings (Kiowa, b. 1952). Oklahoma. Rainbow selvage red and blue wool, imitation elk teeth (bone), brass sequins, brass bells, military patches, ribbons, thread, dyed tooling leather, German silver conchos, spots, and buckle. 26/5646

Wives Honoring Husbands, ca. 1880. Julian Scott Ledger Artist, Kiowa. Paper, ink, colored pencil, 19 x 32 cm. Collection of Charles and Valerie Diker, LD 047.

Carl and Vanessa Jennings at the annual Kiowa Black Leggings Society ceremonials, Anadarko, Oklahoma. Vanessa, a well-known Kiowa artist whose work includes dresses, leggings, cradleboards, shields, dolls, and horse equipment, proudly wears a Battle Dress that she made to honor Native American warriors, in particular her husband Carl.

These men are the reason I feel so strongly about warriors and the Battle Dress. I have never had to jump from an airplane into the heart of enemy territory. I wasn't imprisoned and tortured by the Viet Cong. I didn't have to survive a direct hit from a torpedo as it ripped a hole in the side of a submarine. I didn't drive an ammunition truck through a valley with expert German snipers firing at me, I wasn't left with other Marines on an island with orders to fight the Japanese without additional ammunition or reinforcements. I never landed on a beach with gunfire and land mines exploding all around me. I didn't have to inject myself with anti-nerve gas while fighting Saddam's army. By wearing the Battle Dress, I recognize and honor these sacrifices.... There is a large payment in blood for our freedom. In our Indian culture it is not proper for a man to brag on his war deeds. It is the woman's responsibility to dress and dance to honor him.[38]

Jennings recalls that her great-grandmother wore a Battle Dress made from an enemy flag captured during World War I, while she and her peers wear dresses that incorporate in beadwork the medals, ribbons, or patches earned by their husbands in the Vietnam War. Like the late-nineteenth-century dresses on pp. 132, 135, and 136, the dresses of women honoring male veterans can be red and blue or red and black. Jennings points out that the Kiowa War Mothers, the Purple Heart Club, and other women's auxiliaries wear red and blue, but only the women related to the elite soldiers of the Kiowa Black Leggings Society wear red and black. Indeed, the design of this dress is proprietary to this society, and has been copyrighted. The sleeves are red, and the necklines are beaded in rectangular bands (as the ones in the Kiowa drawing on p. 139 seem to be). Elk teeth and other ornaments, and red aprons and capes may be worn as well. Such contemporary dresses—again, like the Lakota painted dresses—are a very public way of honoring the bravery of fighting men, and the valor and loss of women who have given their husbands and sons to the military.

Women's artistic work has always had deep cultural importance; this is affirmed and highlighted by the traditional stories I have recounted. As Colleen Cutschall relates in her essay in this book, the Lakota have a story about the end of the world in which an old woman's dog undoes her quillwork while she attends to her cooking fire. "As fast as she sews, the dog unravels her work. If she should ever finish her quillwork, the world will end at that instant."[39]

The astonishing display of historical and contemporary women's artistry reassures us that the world probably will not be in danger of ending any time soon. The last word on the subject belongs to one of the Native artists consulted for this book. Keri Jhane Myers eloquently expresses the deep meaning of the garments:

> When I was growing up, these dresses were part of our family. For the women in my family, the buckskin dress is part of our being. Every week in my life, I spent at least two to three days in my own dress, in my own buckskin. And I think that's a defining point to being Native American nowadays, because it's a strong tie to your culture.... For me that's real important, because it's been a marker in my life all the way back to my great-grandmother. I can see that we use those dresses to define ourselves as women. When you have that strong cultural background, when you have a strong tie to your culture, it makes anything that you want to do in the world easy.

WOMEN'S WORK IS NEVER DONE—A VIEW FROM CONTEMPORARY BEADWORKERS

I get up at about four o'clock in the morning. I work from about four till eleven. That's my time when I don't have any interruptions.

—Jackie Parsons (Blackfeet)

I used to get up at two o'clock in the morning and start on an outfit so I could get it done on time and just bead all day long. And if my husband was going to work, why I'd get his breakfast, too, and then he'd leave and I'd just stay at the bead. And I was always, always, and always at it.

—Inez Hubert (Spokane)[40]

We put our work first before we do other things. I have to get up around four o'clock in the morning sometimes to work. Usually that's when I have my best time—from four to six, or whenever the kids get up. Then I tend to them. When they're all off to school or whatever they're doing, I go back to my work. That's how it is just about every day.

—Joyce Growing Thunder Fogarty
(Assiniboine/Sioux)

Blackfeet artist Jackie Parsons, 2005.

Jackie is the first Native chairperson of the Montana Arts Council and a longtime participant in and winner of many awards at the annual Northern Plains Tribal Arts Show and Market in Sioux Falls, South Dakota. In making the new dress that she is wearing, she added basket beads that she had saved from an older dress to the fringe of the yoke. For Jackie, this connects the past to the present.

Sioux two-hide pattern dress with fully beaded yoke,
ca. 1890. South Dakota. Hide, seed beads, sinew.
19/7484

Lakota women prefer beading with "lane stitch,"
also called "lazy stitch," which results in designs
that resemble those made with porcupine quills. By
stringing multiple seed beads on a needle before attaching the thread back down on the hide, this artist
covered a larger area of the yoke faster than if she
had used quills.

NOTES

1. Lakota artist Arthur Amiotte, personal communication; see also Amiotte, "An Appraisal of Sioux Arts," in Arthur Huseboe, *An Illustrated History of the Arts of South Dakota* (Sioux Falls, S.D.: The Center for Western Studies, Augustana College, 1989), 124.

2. See Betty Bastien, *Blackfoot Ways of Knowing: The Worldview of the Siksikaitsitapi.* (Alberta: University of Calgary Press, 2004), 2–5. She cites a Blackfoot term for such knowledge: Kii Nai'tsistomato'k Ai'stamma't-so'tsspi, which means "embodying the knowledge you have been given," or "making knowledge part of the body," 207.

3. Lillian Ackerman, ed., *A Song to the Creator: Traditional Arts of Native American Women of the Plateau* (Norman: University of Oklahoma Press, 1996), 132. The quotation is from a 1992 interview with this contemporary quill- and beadwork artist.

4. James Teit, *Mythology of the Thompson Indians.* Memoirs of the American Museum of Natural History 12, no. 2 (1912): 328, as quoted in Ackerman, *A Song to the Creator,* 105.

5. This is my paraphrase of the original myth published in Clark Wissler, *Societies and Ceremonial Associations in the Oglala Division of the Teton Dakota.* American Museum of Natural History Anthropological Papers 11, no. 1: 93.

6. George Bird Grinnell, *The Cheyenne Indians,* Vol. 1 (New York: Cooper Square Publishers, 1962), 165. See also Alice Marriott, "The Trade Guild of the Southern Cheyenne Women," *Bulletin of the Oklahoma Anthropological Society* 4 (1956): 19–27.

7. Frances Densmore, *Teton Sioux Music,* Bulletin of American Ethnology Bulletin 61 (Washington, D.C.: The Smithsonian Institution). Reprinted as *Teton Sioux Music and Culture* (Lincoln: University of Nebraska Press, 1992), 296.

8. Barbara Tedlock, "The Beautiful and the Dangerous: Zuni Ritual and Cosmology as an Aesthetic System," in Janet C. Berlo and Lee Anne Wilson, eds., *Arts of Africa, Oceania, and the Americas: Selected Readings* (Englewood Cliffs, N.J.: Prentice Hall, 1993), 48–63. [First published in *Conjunctions* 6 (1984): 246–65.]

9. George Catlin, *Letters and Notes on the Manners, Customs, and Conditions of North American Indians,* Vol. 1 (New York: Dover Publications, 1973), 147. [Original edition 1844.]

10. Kate Duncan, "Beadwork on the Plateau," in Robin Wright, ed., *A Time of Gathering: Native Heritage in Washington State* (Seattle: University of Washington Press, 1991), 189–96. The quotations are from pp. 195 and 191, respectively.

11. Unless otherwise noted, all quotations from contemporary artists in this essay derive from interviews conducted with the artists by Emil Her Many Horses and Colleen Cutschall at NMAI in December 2005.

12. See, for example, Frances Wood, *The Silk Road: Two Thousand Years in the Heart of Asia* (Berkeley: University of California Press, 2002).

13. See Theodore Stern, "Columbia River Trade Network," *Handbook of North American Indians,* Vol. 12 (Washington, D.C.: Smithsonian Institution, 1998), 641–52; fur trader Alexander Ross's characterization of the Dalles as an "emporium" is on p. 649. An excellent introduction to the subject of trade and its literature is William Swagerty, "Indian Trade in the Trans-Mississippian West to 1870, *Handbook of North American Indians,* Vol. 4 (Washington, D.C.: Smithsonian Institution, 1988), 351–74.

14. Castle McLaughlin has shown that an early side-fold dress long thought to be "traditional" in style actually reflects the rich array of international goods available on the Plains at the beginning of the nineteenth century. See her "Objects and Identities: Another Look at Lewis and Clark's Side-Fold Dresses," *American Indian Art Magazine* 29, no. 1 (Winter 2003): 76–85.

15. Donald Jackson, ed., *Letters of the Lewis and Clark Expedition,* Vol. 2 (Urbana: University of Illinois Press, 1978), 529.

16. Sample lists of inventories of trade goods, circa 1800, can be found in the Appendices in W. Raymond Wood and Thomas Thiessen, *Early Fur Trade on the Northern Plains* (Norman: University of Oklahoma Press, 1985).

Kiowa three-hide dress, ca. 1910. Oklahoma. Hide, cowrie shells, seed beads, ermine skins, red wool, yellow and green paint, sinew, string. 2/2459

Women sometimes substituted cowries for elk teeth as decoration on dresses. The shape of cowries is close to that of the teeth.

17. James Gibson, *Otter Skins, Boston Ships, and China Goods: The Maritime Fur Trade of the Northwest Coast, 1785–1841* (Montreal: McGill-Queen's University Press, 1992), 9, 228–30.

18. Gibson, 228. According to Richard Conn, the source for Chinese coins in subsequent decades was the influx of Chinese immigrants in Oregon. See "Plateau Native Leather Clothing, Traditional and Modern," in Ackerman, *A Song to the Creator*, 79.

19. Wood and Thiessen, 219.

20. Traders' invoices in St. Louis in 1835 list 600 pounds of vermilion at $1.18 per pound. Just a few years later it was $2.50 per pound. See Charles Hanson, "A Paper of Vermilion," *The Museum of the Fur Trade Quarterly* 7, no. 3 (1971): 1–3 and "Paint Pigments in the Fur Trade," vol. 17, no. 4 (1981): 1–5.

21. Swagerty, "Indian Trade," 367.

22. Stern, "Columbia River Trade Network," 649.

23. For illustration, see Janet C. Berlo and Ruth Phillips, *Native North American Art* (Oxford: Oxford University Press, 1998), figure 18.

24. Garrick Mallery, *Picture-Writing of the American Indians*, Vol. 1 (New York: Dover Reprints, 1972), 325. [Original publication date, 1893.] On the trade in Navajo blankets, see Joe Ben Wheat, "American Indian Weaving: Early Trade and Commerce Before the Curio Shop," *Oriental Rug Review* 8, no. 4 and 5 (1988).

25. See Eulalie Bonar, ed., *Woven by the Grandmothers: Nineteenth-Century Navajo Textiles from the National Museum of the American Indian* (Washington, D.C.: Smithsonian Institution Press, 1996), Plate 21, and pp. 128, 187. Da-Cost Smith recounted his travels among the Lakota in *Indian Experiences* (Caldwell, Idaho: The Caxton Printers), 1943.

26. See George P. Horse Capture and Joseph D. Horse Capture, *Beauty, Honor, and Tradition: The Legacy of Plains Indian Shirts* (Minneapolis and Washington, D.C.: Smithsonian's National Museum of the American Indian and the Minneapolis Institute of Arts, 2001) and Janet C. Berlo, ed., *Plains Indian Drawings 1865–1935: Pages from a Visual History* (New York: The American Federation of Arts, 1996).

27. George Bird Grinnell, *The Cheyenne Indians*, Vol. 1 (New York: Cooper Square Publishers, 1962), 159–161.

28. As told to Gilbert Wilson (ca. 1910), in Carolyn Gilman and Mary Jane Schneider, *The Way to Independence: Memoirs of a Hidatsa Indian Family, 1840–1920* (St. Paul: Minnesota Historical Society Press, 1987), 57.

29. Transcript of interview, NMAI, December 2005, reel 4–6.

30. Alice Marriott and Carol Rachlin, *Dance Around the Sun: The Life of Mary Little Bear Inkanish, Cheyenne* (New York: Thomas Y. Crowell Co., 1977), 5.

31. See Marsha Bol, "Beaded Costume of the Early Reservation Era," in Janet C. Berlo and Lee Anne Wilson, eds., *Arts of Africa, Oceania and the Americas: Selected Readings* (Englewood Cliffs, N.J.: Prentice Hall, 1993), 363–70.

32. Raymond DeMallie, "Male and Female in Traditional Lakota Culture," in Patricia Albers and Beatrice Medicine, eds., *The Hidden Half: Studies of Plains Indian Women* (Lanham, Md.: University Press of America, 1983), 247. See also James Walker, *Lakota Belief and Ritual*, Raymond DeMallie and Elaine Jahner, eds. (Lincoln: University of Nebraska Press, 1980), 165–6.

33. As recorded by Robert Lowie, *Myths and Traditions of the Crow* [Anthropological Papers # 25] (New York: American Museum of Natural History, 1922), 119–26.

34. Walter McClintock, "Painted Tipis and Picture-Writing of the Blackfoot Indians, Part 2," *The Masterkey* 10, no. 5 (1936): 176, and figs. 16 and 17.

35. Evan Maurer, ed., *Visions of the People* (Minneapolis: The Minneapolis Institute of Arts, 1992), object nos. 154 and 155, pp. 198–99; object no. 240, p. 247.

36. Frances Densmore, *Teton Sioux Music*, Bulletin of American Ethnology Bulletin 61 (Washington, D.C.: The Smithsonian Institution). Reprinted as *Teton Sioux Music and Culture* (Lincoln: University of Nebraska Press, 1992), 367. Densmore includes illustrations of a Lakota named Silent Woman wearing such a dress, and front and back views of the dress (Plates 54 and 55).

37. Maurer, *Visions of the People*, object no. 200, p. 223. The only other examples known to me are an oddly painted dress (erroneously called a man's shirt) in Judy Thomp-

son, *The North American Indian Collection* (Berne, Switzerland: The Berne Historical Museum, 1977), Figure 102, which is said to be Sioux but does not resemble Sioux painting. One earlier Lakota buckskin and beaded dress owned by Pretty White Cow at Standing Rock Reservation is painted with scenes of women hunting and butchering animals. See Maurer, object no. 245, p. 250.

38. Vanessa Jennings, "The Tradition of the Kiowa Battle Dress," *Whispering Wind* 32, no. 3 (2002): 8–16. Originally published in the *Anadarko Daily News*, Oct. 12–13, 1991.

39. William Powers, *Oglala Religion* (Lincoln: University of Nebraska Press, 1977), 85.

40. Ackerman, *A Song to the Creator*, 118.

Comanche high-top moccasins, ca. 1890. Oklahoma. Hide, seed beads, silver metallic spots, yellow and red paint, rawhide, sinew. 2/1501

"Horse culture was the main way of life. Young women, likely sisters, used to ride double on the horses to go swimming and berry picking."

—Joyce Growing Thunder Fogarty (Assiniboine/Sioux)

Northern Cheyenne girls on horseback, ca. 1900. Montana. Photographer unknown. P07814

Contributors

JANET CATHERINE BERLO is Professor of Art History and Visual and Cultural Studies at the University of Rochester, in western New York. She is the author of numerous books on Native American art history, including *Native North American Art* (with Ruth Phillips, Oxford, 1997), *Plains Indian Drawings 1865–1935: Pages from a Visual History* (Abrams, 1996), and *Spirit Beings and Sun Dancers: Black Hawk's Vision of a Lakota World* (Braziller, 2000). She has received fellowships from the Guggenheim Foundation, the Getty Trust, and the National Endowment for the Humanities in support of her work.

COLLEEN CUTSCHALL (Oglala Lakota), co-curator of the National Museum of the American Indian exhibition *Identity by Design: Tradition, Change, and Celebration in Native Women's Dresses*, is an artist whose preferred mediums include painting and installation. Cutschall, who once studied under noted painter Oscar Howe (Yanktonai Sioux, 1915–1983), has had numerous solo and group exhibitions and is the sculptural designer of *Spirit Warriors – Little Bighorn Aboriginal Memorial* (2003) at the Little Bighorn Battlefield National Monument in Montana. She is presently a professor and Chair of the Visual and Aboriginal Art Department at Brandon University, Brandon, Manitoba, Canada. Cutschall has produced many publications and lectures on Native issues and art. She is a recipient of a Rockefeller Foundation Research Residency at the Bellagio Study and Conference Center in Italy in 2006.

EMIL HER MANY HORSES (Oglala Lakota), co-curator of the National Museum of the American Indian (NMAI) exhibition *Identity by Design: Tradition, Change, and Celebration in Native Women's Dresses*, is an associate curator at NMAI. He was lead curator for one of the inaugural permanent exhibitions at NMAI in Washington, D.C., *Our Universes: Traditional Knowledge Shapes Our World*, which focuses on indigenous cosmologies—worldviews and philosophies related to the creation and the order of the universe—and the spiritual relationship between humankind and the natural world. Her Many Horses, who specializes in Northern and Southern Plains culture, is an accomplished beadwork artist and winner of the 2001 Best of Show category for his tribute to the Lakota Sioux Vietnam Veterans at the Northern Plains Tribal Arts Show. Her Many Horses served as co-editor of *A Song for the Horse Nation: Horses in Native American Cultures* (2006).

ELIZABETH WOODY (Warm Springs-Yakama/Navajo), poet, received her BA at The Evergreen State College. She lives in Portland, Oregon, and is Director of the Indigenous Leadership Program at Ecotrust, a nonprofit organization that promotes conservation-based development.

PROJECT CONSULTANTS

The National Museum of the American Indian invited six celebrated Native women artists whose many skills include designing dresses to come to the museum in Washington, D.C., in December 2005 for a workshop to discuss the museum's dress collection and Native dressmaking. The wisdom and experience of Joyce Growing Thunder Fogarty (Assiniboine/Sioux), Juanita Growing Thunder Fogarty (Assiniboine/Sioux), Gladys Jefferson (Crow), Keri Jhane Myers (Comanche), Jamie Okuma (Luiseño/Shoshone-Bannock), and Jackie Parsons (Blackfeet) reveal the dresses presented in this book as reflections of a woman's identity—her tribal and family traditions and individual artistic skill and expression.

Additional Native artists, dancers, and educators, including Rebecca Brady (Cheyenne/Sac and Fox), Jodi Gillette (Hunkpapa Lakota), Vanessa Jennings (Kiowa), Pamela S. Woodis (Jicarilla Apache), and Georgianna Old Elk (Assiniboine), among others, also generously shared their knowledge.

Sioux two-hide pattern dress with fully beaded yoke, ca. 1910. Probably North Dakota or South Dakota. Hide, seed beads, sinew. 2/5800

When creating a dress that requires beading a large area, an experienced artist knows to buy enough beads to complete her work. If she runs out, it is very difficult to find the same color because dye lots used to make beads differ. In past times, however, if a dressmaker ran out of beads while making a garment, she continued on with the closest color she could obtain, as can be seen in the color variation in the beaded yoke of this dress.

Credits

Sioux beaded leggings and moccasins, ca. 1880. Hide, seed beads, green paint, rawhide, and sinew.
19/3706

Index

Page numbers in **boldface** indicate pages
with illustrations.

A

achievement and honor, dresses signifying,
90, 123–40
adolescent girls entering womanhood,
69–77
adoption of girl children, **66**, 67
aesthetics of dress, 103–8
American flag designs, **48**, 49, **50**, 89
ancestral knowledge, dresses embodying, 97
animal tail on two-hide dresses
imitated on cloth dresses, **128**
life and generativity referenced by, **98**
replaced with U-shaped design, **40**, **42**, 43
Apache
Changing Woman or White Shell Woman,
70
Jicarilla Apache Keesda Ceremony, 70
Sunrise Ceremony, 70
White Mountain Apache girl's cape and
skirt, **9**, **71**
Arapaho
cloth dress, **75**
Ghost Dance dress, **86**, **87**, 89
two-hide pattern dress with fully beaded
yoke, **14–15**, **51**
woman at U.S. Indian Congress, Trans-
Mississippi and International Exposition, **124**
Arikara two-hide dress, **29**, **93**
Assiniboine-style modern dress by Joyce
Growing Thunder Fogarty, **46**
awl case, beaded, Yankton Sioux, **1**, **77**

B

bags. *See* purses and bags
battle dresses, 134–40
Hunkpapa Lakota (Sioux), **134**, **135**
Kiowa, **106**, 137–40, **138**
Mandan dress, documentation of, 137
Sioux, **131**, **132**, **136**, **137**
beads and beading, 43–49. *See also* specific
styles, stitches, and types of beads
color variations, 151
cosmopolitan influences on, 98
male beadworkers, 134
reservation confinement, beading as
means of dealing with, 46, 49
spiritual elements of, 44
three bands on Cheyenne three-hide
dresses, **56**, 57
trade and indigenous sources, 26
Berlo, Janet Catherine, 96–147, **149**
Big Eyes, wife of, 134
Bigcrane, Joanne, 98
Black Leggings Society (Kiowa), 140
Blackfeet
cloth dresses, **46**, **81**, **84**, **107**, **119**
Headdress or War Bonnet Society, 85
Kii Nai'tsistomato'k Ai'stamma'tso'tsspi,
145n2
two-hide dress, 33, **34**, **35**, **114**
upright feather bonnets, **84**, **85**
War Mothers Society, 85
woman in decorated wool dress, **81**
woman in upright feather bonnet, **85**
blood
menstrual, 77
as Sun Dance offering, 73

blue breast beading, 43
Blunt Horn, John, 18
Bodmer, Karl
    Chan-Chä-Uiá-Teüin, Teton Sioux Woman
        (1833–39), 21, 24
    Piegan Blackfeet man wearing Navajo
        blanket and Pueblo silver pendant,
        painting of, 120
Brady, Cheyenne, 57, 60, 61, 88
Brady, Jon, 57, 58, 60, 61, 88
Brady, Rebecca, 57, 57–60, 88
Buffalo Bird Woman, 123

C

canvas used for three-hide dresses during
    World War II, 57
Catlin, George, 107
cedar tree, sacred, 87, 89
Chan-Chä-Uiá-Teüin, 21, 24
Changing Woman (Apache), 70
Cheyenne
    cloth dress (ca. 1910?), 96–97, 111
    Comanche three-hide dresses compared,
        92
    girl children
        elaborate beaded dress and breastplate,
            126
        elk tooth cloth dresses, 126
        modern cloth dress and accessories,
            60, 61
    horseback, girls on, 148
    purses, 59, 60
    Quillwork Society, 123
    three-hide dress and accessories, modern,
        57–59
    three-hide dress, ca. 1930, 10, 56, 57
    woman using smoother on quillwork, 77
    women's artistic guilds, 102
children. See girl children
Chinese coins, 104, 114
Clark, William, 111
cloth dresses, 60–62
    Arapaho
        cloth dress, 75
        Ghost Dance dress, 86, 87, 89
    battle dresses. See battle dresses
    Blackfeet cloth dresses, 46, 81, 84, 107, 119
    broadcloth, 62
    canvas used for three-hide dresses during
        World War II, 57
    Cheyenne, 60, 61, 96–97, 111, 126
    Crow, 38, 39, 82, 122

with elk tooth decoration. See elk teeth
    Ghost Dance dresses, 86, 87, 89
    hide-pattern dress, imitating, 119
    Hunkpapa Lakota (Sioux) cloth dresses, 3,
        50, 134, 135
    Kiowa cloth dress, 26
    Mandan, 76
    modern dresses, 62
    "saved-list" white edge on woolen cloth,
        26, 50, 60, 116, 117
    Sioux, 116, 117, 131, 132, 136, 137
    woolen cloth used for dressmaking, 26,
        60–62
coins, Chinese, 104, 114
collaborative efforts, 133–34
Comanche
    color symbolism, 81
    moccasins, 147
    Mumsookawa, Chief, and two wives, 90
    otterskin caps, 90, 91
    three-hide dresses, 92, 112–13, 115
Conn, Richard, 28
contemporary dresses. See modern dresses
cosmopolitanism of dress design, 97, 109–21
    as aesthetic preference, 103–4
    beadwork, influences on, 98
    incorporation of trade goods into dress
        design, 22–27
    intertribal influences, 32, 33
    map of trade routes and trade centers, 110
    women's involvement in trade, 120
cotton. See cloth dresses
cottonwood tree, sacred, 73
cowrie shells, 50, 60, 145
cradleboards, 78, 79, 80
cross-gender collaboration, 134, 137
Crow
    cloth elk tooth dress, 122
    cloth imitation elk tooth dress, 128
    horseback, women on, 38
    modern cloth elk tooth dresses, 38, 39
    Tobacco Society, 81–84, 82, 83
    transitional two-hide elk tooth dress, 2,
        36, 37
    woman with baby in decorated cradle-
        board, 78
culture and identity. See dresses as expres-
    sions of culture and identity
Curtis, Edward, 104
cut glass beads, 17, 28
Cutschall, Colleen, 64–93, 140, 149, 149–50
    The Pregnant Grandfather (1988), 72

Sisterwolf in Her Moon (1992), 74
Voice in the Blood (1990), 73

D

dancing and dancing dresses
    Apache Sunrise Ceremony, 70
    battle dresses, 137
    Brady, Rebecca, **57–59**
    Crow Fair celebrations, **39**
    Ghost Dance, **86,** 86–89, **87**
    Gillette, Jodi, **20,** 21, 24
    at NMAI National Powwow, **20, 21, 105**
    Old Elk, Georgianna, **52, 53**
    Sun Dance, 49, 62, 73–74, **74,** 126
    three-hide dance dresses with fringe, **54**
    War Bonnet or Headdress Society
      (Blackfeet), 85
    war implements and trophies, women
      with, **39,** 137, **139**
    "Women's Traditional" competitions, 40
dentalium shells, 24, 60, 102, 104, 108, 114,
    116, 117
dew claws, 24
dog unraveling quillwork, 65, 140
Double Woman (Lakota), 102, 130
dreams, 12, 22, 52, 95, 103, 130
dresses as expressions of culture and iden-
    tity, 11–13, 62, 140–41
    adolescent girls entering womanhood,
      69–77
    adult women and women's societies or
      guilds, 77–85, 102, 140
    aesthetics of dress, 103–8
    ancestral knowledge, dresses embody-
      ing, 97
    children's ceremonies and rituals,
      67–68
    collaborative efforts, 133–34
    cosmopolitanism. *See* cosmopolitanism
      of dress design
    elders, women as, 90
    grandmothers' cultural and symbolic
      roles, 65–67
    Her Many Horses, Emil, grandmothers
      of, 16–18
    honor and achievement, dresses signi-
      fying, 90, 123–40
    reservation confinement, beading and
      dressmaking as means of dealing
      with, 46, 49, 130
    spirituality. *See* spiritual functions of
      women's dress

Dubin, Louis Sherr, 28
Duncan, Kate, 107–8

E

ear-piercing, 73
earrings
    Cheyenne, **59**
    Nez Perce, **6–7,** 31
    Sicangu Lakota (Sioux), **116, 117**
    Wishram woman, **104**
eclecticism of dress design. *See* cosmopoli-
    tanism of dress design
elders, women as, 90
elk teeth, 37–39, 123–26
    cowries substituted for, 145
    Crow elk tooth dresses, **2,** 36–**39, 122, 128**
    eyeteeth only used as decoration, 17, 41
    girl children, elk tooth dresses made for,
      126
    imitation elk teeth, **36, 37,** 39, **128**
    wedding dresses, elk tooth dresses as, 126
Erdrich, Heid E., 11–12
eyeteeth, elk tooth decoration made only
    from, 17, 41

F

face painting
    for Hunka (Making of Relatives) Cere-
      mony, **66,** 67
    Keesda Ceremony (Jicarilla Apache), 70
    at naming ceremony, 68
Falling Star or White Buffalo Calf Woman
    (Lakota), 70, 73
Feder, Norman, 22
five hides used for fringes on contemporary
    three-hide dance dresses, 54
flag designs used on dresses, **48,** 49, **50,** 89,
    140
flat gourd stitch beading, **92**
flesh offerings from upper arms, women
    giving, 73
Fletcher, Alice, 69
floral beadwork style of Red River Métis
    people, spread of, 98
Fogarty, Joyce Growing Thunder, **19, 43,**
    43–44, **44, 130,** 131, 141, 150
Fogarty, Juanita Growing Thunder, **19, 43,**
    43–44, 49, 62, 89, 150
Fourth of July celebrations, dresses worn for,
    49, **50**
fringe

three-hide dance dresses with, **54**
two-hide Plateau-style dresses with, *103*

G

gender boundaries, working across, 134, 137
Ghost Dance, **86–87**, 86–89
Gillette, Jodi, **20–21**, 21, 24
girl children
    adolescent girls entering womanhood,
        69–77
    adoption of, **66**, 67
    ceremonies and rituals associated with,
        67–68
    Cheyenne
        elaborate beaded dress and breastplate,
            126
        elk tooth dresses, **126**
        modern girl's cloth dress and acces-
            sories, **60–61**
    Sicangu Lakota (Sioux) dress, moccasins,
        and leggings, **127**
    White Mountain Apache girl's cape and
        skirt, **9**, **71**
give-away ceremonies, 17–18, 126, 130, **131**
Give Away Horses dress, Joyce Growing Thun-
    der Fogarty, 130, **131**
Goodwill, Danita, **105**
grandmothers
    cultural and symbolic roles of, 65–67
    Her Many Horses, Emil, 15–18
Gray Hawk, Ben and Josephine, 130, 131
Grinnell, George Bird, 123
guilds or societies for women, 77–85, 102,
    140

H

Hale, Tawny, **105**
hats. *See* headdresses
headdresses
    Blackfeet upright feather bonnets, **84**, **85**
    Blackfeet War Bonnet or Headdress Soci-
        ety, 85
    Cheyenne accessories, Rebecca and Jon
        Brady, **57–61**, **88**
    heart design headdress, Keri Jhane Myers,
        80
    otterskin caps, **90**, **91**
    Wishram woman, **104**
    Yakama basket hat, **31**
heart design, **80**, 81
Her Many Horses, Emil, 15–63, **150**

Her Many Horses, Emily, 17–18
Heye, George Gustav, 22
honor and achievement, dresses signifying,
    90, 123–40
horseback, women and girls on, **38**, **148**
Hubert, Inez, 141
Hunka (Making of Relatives) Ceremony
    (Sioux), **66**, 67, **68**
Hunkpapa Lakota (Sioux) dresses, *3*, *50*, 134,
    135

I

identity and culture. *See* dresses as expres-
    sions of culture and identity
*Identity by Design: Tradition, Change, and Cele-
    bration in Native Women's Dresses*, NMAI, 11,
    18, 66
imitation elk teeth, **36–37**, 39
"The Invisible Dress," Elizabeth Woody, 94
Iraq War, 85, 139
Ishna Ta Awi Cha Lowan (preparing for
    womanhood ceremony), Lakota, 74

J

Jefferson, Gladys, **19**, 39, 67, 81, 123, **125**,
    150
Jennings, Vanessa, 54, 57, 137–40, **139**
Jennys, Susan, 33
Jicarilla Apache Keesda Ceremony, 70

K

Keesda Ceremony (Jicarilla Apache), 70
Kii Nai'tsistomato'k Ai'stamma'tso'tsspi, 145n2
Kiowa
    battle dresses, **106**, 137–40, **138**
    cloth dress, **26**
    societies for relatives of war veterans, 140
    three-hide dresses, **41**, **55**, 57, **144**
    war implements and trophies, women
        dancing with, *137*, **139**

L

La Flesche, Francis, 69
lake or water, blue beaded yokes symboliz-
    ing, 43, **47**, 73, 98, **100**
Lakota. *See also* Sicangu Lakota
    creation stories, 73
    Double Woman, 102, 130
    Hunkpapa Lakota (Sioux) dresses, *3*, *50*,
        134, **135**
    Maka, 73

pipe, 73, **87**, 89
  White Buffalo Calf Woman (Wohpe or
    Falling Star), 70, 73
  Wounded Knee massacre, 86
lazy-stitch or lane-stitch bead- and quill-
    work, 37, 104, 142
leggings
  Crow elk tooth cloth dress, leggings, and
    moccasins, **122**
  Kiowa Black Leggings Society, 140
  Sicangu Lakota (Sioux) girl's dress, moc-
    casins, and leggings, **127**
  Sioux beaded leggings and moccasins,
    153
Lessard, Rosemary, 22
Little Bear Inkanish, Mary, 126
Lone Bear, Alice, 120, **124**
Lyon, Rebecca, 11

M

Máh-to-tóh-pa, Catlin's portrait of, 107, **108**
Maka (Lakota), 73
Making of Relatives (Hunka) Ceremony
    (Sioux), **66**, 67, **68**
male beadworkers and narrative painters,
    134, 137
Mandan
  battle dress, documentation of, 137
  cloth dress, **76**
Mark of Honor, **69**
Mathews, Susie (Blunt Horn) and Louis, 17
McClintock, Walter, 134
menstruation, 74–77
moccasins
  Comanche, **147**
  Crow Tobacco Society, **83**
  with fully beaded soles, 17, 126
  Ghost Dance, **86**
  intertribal trade in, 120
  Ishna Ta Awi Cha Lowan (preparing for
    womanhood ceremony), Lakota, 74
  Old Elk, Georgianna, **53**
  Sicangu Lakota (Sioux) girl's moccasins
    and leggings, **127**
  Sioux beaded leggings and moccasins,
    153
modern dresses
  Brady, Rebecca and Jon, **57–61**
  cloth used for, 62
  Fogarty, Joyce Growing Thunder, **46**, 130,
    131
  Gillette, Jodi, **20–21**, 21, 24
  Jennings, Vanessa, **106**, **138**

Myers, Keri Jhane, **80**, 81, **91**
  Okuma, Jamie, **33**
  Old Elk, Georgianna, 52, **52–53**
  Parsons, Jackie, **141**
Momaday, N. Scott, 15
Mourning Dove, 77, 80
multidimensional aesthetic of dress, 103–7
Mumsookawa, Chief, and two wives, **90**
Myers, Keri Jhane, 18, **19**, 54, **80**, 81, 90, **91**,
    109, 123, 132, 140, 150

N

naming ceremony, 17–18, 67, 68, 73
National Museum of the American Indian
    (NMAI)
      as cultural center, 11
      National Powwow, **20**, **21**, **105**, **129**
Native American Church, **57–61**, **88**, 89
Navajo blankets, intertribal trade in, 120, **121**
  necklaces
    Nez Perce, **6–7**, **31**
    Sicangu Lakota (Sioux) choker, **116**, **117**
Nez Perce
  eclectic styles of, 33
  two-hide pattern dress with fully beaded
    yoke, **98**, **99**
NMAI. *See* National Museum of the
    American Indian
Nootka people, 114

O

O-o-be, **41**
Okuma, Jamie, **19**, 28, **33**, 123, 150
Old Elk, Dora, **129**
Old Elk, Georgianna, 52, 53
"Old One" (Shuswap), 102
Oldman, W. O., 22
Omaha, Mark of Honor tattoo used by, **69**
One Star, Annabelle, 17
otterskin caps, **90**, **91**

P

Parker, Chief Quanah, 89
Parsons, Jackie, 18, **19**, 33, 62, 85, **141**, 150
peyote, 57, **88**, 89
Piegan Blackfeet man wearing Navajo blan-
    ket and Pueblo silver pendant, Bodmer's
    painting of, 120
pipe in Lakota ceremonies, 73, **87**, 89
pony beads, **22–23**, 23, **25**, 26, 28, 33, 46
porcupine quills. *See* quillwork
Pourier, Grace, **16**, 17

The *Pregnant Grandfather*, 1988, Colleen
    Cutschall, **72**
puberty and puberty ceremonies, 69–77
purses and bags
    cosmopolitanism of design, aesthetic
        preference for, 103
    modern Cheyenne, **59, 60, 88**
    Yakama, **30**

Q

quillwork
    dog unraveling, 65, **140**
    Double Woman (Lakota), 102, **130**
    side-fold dress, 22–23, **22–23, 25**
    Sioux robes, **64–65,** 65, **66,** 67, **68**

R

red materials and pigments, 114, **118**
Red River Métis people, spread of floral
    beadwork style of, 98
reservation confinement, beading and dress
    making as means of dealing with, 46, 49,
        130
Ridington, Robin, 69
robes
    Sioux robe for Hunka ceremony, 67, **68**
    Sioux robe with beaded detail, **64–65, 66**
Russian or Siberian beads, 28, **31, 103**

S

Santa Fe Indian Market, 14, 42
"saved-list" white edge on woolen cloth, 26,
    50, 60, **116–17**
Schemitzun Powwow, Connecticut, 57, 109
seed beads, 26, 28, 46
"She Dances," Heid E. Erdrich, 11–12
Sherman, Geraldine, 66–67
Shoshone
    eclectic styles of, **32, 33**
    two-hide dress with fully beaded yoke, **32**
Shuster, Sally, 103–4, **104**
Shuswap, 102
Siberian or Russian beads, 28, **31, 103**
Sicangu Lakota (Sioux)
    earrings and choker, **116, 117**
    girl's dress, **137**
    moccasins with fully beaded soles, 16
    Sun Dancers, **74**
    two-hide pattern dress with fully beaded
        yoke, **47**
side-fold dresses, 21–24

Bodmer, Karl, *Chan-Chä-Uiá-Teüin, Teton
    Sioux Woman* (1833–39), **20,** 24
Gillette, Jodi, modern adaptation by,
    20–21, 21, 24
pattern diagram, 23
Sioux side-fold dress, **22–23,** 22–24, **25**
Sinte Gleska (Spotted Tail), wife of, **14**
Sioux. *See also* Lakota; Sicangu Lakota
    battle dresses, **131, 132, 136, 137**
    beaded leggings and moccasins, **153**
    Chan-Chä-Uiá-Teüin, Teton Sioux Woman
        1833–39, Karl Bodmer, **21,** 24
    cloth dresses, **116, 117, 131, 132, 136, 137**
    Hunka (Making of Relatives) Ceremony,
        66, 67, **68**
    Hunkpapa Lakota (Sioux) dresses, **3, 50,**
        134, 135
    moccasins, intertribal trade in, 120
    robes, **64–68**
    side-fold dress, **22–23,** 22–24, **25**
    two-hide dresses
        with American Flag motif fully beaded
            yoke, **48,** 49, **151**
        with fully beaded yoke (ca. 1865), **4, 5,**
            14, 15
        with fully beaded yoke (ca. 1890), **142,**
            143
        with fully beaded yoke (ca. 1900), **100,**
            101
        with fully beaded yoke (ca. 1910), **151**
        transitional style dresses, 39–40, **40, 42**
        Yankton Sioux beaded awl case, **1,** 77
Sisterwolf in Her Moon, 1992, Colleen
    Cutschall, **74**
Smith, DaCost, 120
smoothers used on quillwork, 77
societies or guilds for women, 77–85, 102,
    140
sound, dresses producing, 24, 62, 107
spiritual functions of women's dress, 98–102
    dreams, 12, 22, 52, 95, 103, 130
    Ghost Dance dresses, **86–87,** 86–89
    inseparability of sacred and secular
        realms, 102
    Native American Church, **57–61, 88,** 89
    puberty ceremonies, 69–77
Sun Dance, 49, 62, 73–74, **74,** 126
Sunrise Ceremony (Apache), 70

T

tattoo of Mark of Honor, **69**
Tedlock, Barbara, 103

thimbles used as decorative elements, **81, 84, 85, 107,** 114, **119**
three-hide dresses, 54–60
    canvas used during World War II, 57
    Cheyenne
        three-hide dress and accessories, modern, **57–59**
        three-hide dress (ca. 1930), **10, 56,** 57
    Comanche, **92, 112–13, 115**
    five hides used for fringes on contemporary Southern-style dance dresses, 54
    fringed dancing dresses, **54**
    Kiowa three-hide dresses, **41, 55,** 57
    pattern diagram, **54**
    two-hide transitional style dresses made from three hides, 40
tin cones, 24, **25**
Tobacco Society (Crow), 81–84, **82, 83**
trade and dress design. *See* cosmopolitanism of dress design
turtle design, 43, 52, 67, 76, 88, 98, 100
two-hide dresses, 28–33
    animal tail on
        imitated on cloth dresses, **128**
        life and generativity referenced by, **98**
        replaced with U-shaped design, **40, 42,** 43
    Arapaho, **14–15, 51**
    Arikara, **29, 93**
    Blackfeet, 33, **34, 35, 114**
    Crow transitional two-hide elk tooth dress, **2, 36, 37**
    pattern diagram, **29**
    Shoshone, **32**
    Sicangu Lakota (Sioux), **47**
    Sioux. *See under* Sioux
    three-hides, two-hide transitional style dresses made from, 40
    transitional styles, 37–52
    Yakama, **6–7, 30, 31, 103**

U

upper arms, women giving flesh offerings from, 73
Ute dresses, eclectic style of, 33

V

vermilion, 114, **118,** 146n20
Vietnam War and battle dresses, 137, **139,** 140
Voice in the Blood, 1990, Colleen Cutschall, 73

W

War Bonnet or Headdress Society (Blackfeet), 85
war implements and trophies, women dancing with, **39,** 137, **139**
War Mothers Society
    Blackfeet, 85
    Kiowa, 140
water or lake, blue beaded yokes symbolizing, 43, **47,** 73, 98, **100**
The Way to Rainy Mountain, N. Scott Momaday, 15
West, W. Richard, Jr., 11–13
White Buffalo Calf Woman (Lakota), 70, 73
White Horse, Dorothy, 57
White Mountain Apache girl's cape and skirt, **9, 71**
White Shell Woman (Apache), 70
Wild West Shows, 49
Wishram woman, **104**
Wissler, Clark, 77
Wives Honoring Husbands (ca. 1880), Julian Scott Ledger Artist drawing, **139**
Wohpe or White Buffalo Calf Woman (Lakota), 70, 73
Woodis, Pamela, 70
Woody, Elizabeth, "The Invisible Dress," 94, 150
woolen cloth
    used as decoration, 24, 33, 35, 114, **128**
    used for dressmaking, 26, 60–62. *See also* cloth dresses
World War I and battle dresses, 137, 140
World War II
    battle dresses and, 137
    canvas used for three-hide dresses during, 57
    War Mothers Society (Blackfeet), 85
Wounded Knee massacre, 86
Wovoka, 86

Y

Yakama
    basket hat, **31**
    earrings and necklace, **6–7, 31**
    purse, **30**
    two hide dresses, **6–7, 30, 31, 103**
Yankton Sioux beaded awl case, **1, 77**
yokes, beaded, 17, 40, 98

Z

Zuni aesthetics, 103